Learn Hypnosis

How To Hypnotize Anyone Safely

Paul J Hunter

Disclaimer

The information herein is offered for information purposes solely, and is universal as so

The presentation of the information is without contract or any type of guarantee assurance.

The information included herein is stated to be truthful and consistent, in that any liability,

in terms of inattention or otherwise, by any usage or abuse of any policies, processes or
directions contained is the solitary and utter responsibility of the recipient reader.

Under no circumstances will any legal responsibility or blame be held against the author for
any reparation, damages or monetary loss due to the information herein, either directly
or indirectly.

Contents

This book is dedicated to woman that I am lucky enough
to share my life with, Dorraine,
who is the most beautiful, kind-hearted, giving person.
She inspires me every day to be a better person.
Paul Hunter, May 26th, 2022

Preface

Hi, my name is Paul Hunter and I am a Clinical Hypnotherapist based in Cork, Ireland. I first encountered hypnosis as a 34 year old because of my 50-a-day smoking habit. I'd been smoking for the best part of 15 years and I was really starting to notice the effects on my health – getting out of breath really easily, coughing a lot – all of the usual symptoms.

I tried numerous things to quit. Firstly I tried willpower and the longest I lasted was about nine days until the craving eventually nearly drove me mad and I just gave in and went back to being a smoker. I tried patches, gums........you name it, I probably tried it, and to no avail.

Then a friend of mine suggested hypnosis and, honestly, I thought it was the most hare-brained idea of all. How could a hypnotist do what some of the world's leading names in nicotine replacement products couldn't? But I was at the end of my tether and I (reluctantly) gave in and went and booked an appointment.

As I was sitting there listening to the hypnotherapist speaking to me (before I was hypnotised), I was even thinking to myself "this is such a waste of time and money

– it'll never work". And I went into hypnosis and emerged from trance about an hour later, admittedly feeling very relaxed, but not too sure if I was really a non-smoker. I wasn't aware of any "magic" having happened and didn't really feel that much different.

I decided that I'd just wait and see if I got a craving. That was 22 years ago and I haven't had a craving at any time during those 22 years. At first, I was just pleasantly surprised but as it sank in a couple of months later that I really was finally free of my old addiction, I couldn't help but feel completely blown away.

When I look back on it now, hypnosis has probably saved my life because I know of people who smoked a similar amount to me that developed emphysema, heart disease and even lung cancer. And to be brutally honest, only for that hypnosis session, I could have contracted any of those horrible illnesses and possibly may have died from it. It doesn't take a rocket scientist to work out that a 50-a-day habit is bound to have some serious effect sometime in a person's life.

Because of my amazing experience, I just had to know more about this simple but powerful thing called hypnosis. I wanted to know what else was possible. So I trained to be a hypnotherapist and now I regularly meet clients who want to change their lives.

My clients include smokers, people who want to lose weight, overcome fears of things like spiders, heights, public speaking, etc., people who have chronic anxiety, people who suffer from sexual problems (both male and female), and many more anxiety-related issues.

The great thing about hypnosis is that there is always something new to learn. Each client teaches me to be more flexible in how I interact with them. For a beginner in hypnosis, there is much to be fascinated by and there is a natural temptation to run before you can walk.

If I could offer some advice from my own experience, take your time to practice each step. Become elegant and effortless in how you develop rapport with your subject (or client). When you induce hypnosis, be calm and in control, and always know what to do when the unexpected happens as it often does. The more confident you are, the more your hypnotic subject will trust you and follow you as you lead them into hypnosis.

Don't worry if you are not confident now – I was really nervous when I did my first hypnotic induction. As a matter of fact, my first ever client was a medical doctor who wanted to stop smoking – talk about pressure! But now that I look back on that day I do so with smile on my face. I think it was great to have had a baptism of fire!

By now, I have hypnotised thousands of people and it's become effortless. But it only became effortless with practice. Take the time to put in the practice and you'll become really good at it too.

A WORD OF CAUTION – the scope of this book is purely to show you how to gain rapport with a client and learn how to induce a state of hypnosis. That's all!

I have described above some of the work I do with clients and some of the issues that I deal with. What I am describing is hypnotherapy. Hypnotherapy is what you do when you have your client in hypnosis and requires significant study and practice to be able to do it safely and in the best interests of your client. This book does not train you in hypnotherapy and it important to realise that. The scope of this book is purely and simply to teach you the skills necessary to induce hypnosis in a person.

DO NOT attempt to do therapy with a person in hypnosis when you do not know what you are doing. Make sure you read the chapter on "Hypnotizing Others - Doing It Safely" before you attempt your first hypnotic induction.

FINALLY.....

I wish you all of the best in your study of this fascinating subject of hypnosis. It has become my all-consuming passion. I just can't get enough – I spend my whole day hypnotising people and even when I go to bed at night, my bed-time reading is all about hypnosis. Hypnosis is a powerful tool for good in our world. Use it wisely and safely and you'll find it to be immensely rewarding, both for yourself, and for others too.

FREE GIFT
Before you begin learning about hypnosis and how to hypnotize anyone safely, I believe you must first experience hypnosis yourself. You must know what it feels like to be in a hypnotic trance.

With that in mind I would really like to offer you a **FREE HYPNOSIS MP3** called **Deep Relaxation-**. This is a full length hypnosis recording which will guide you into a trance state, give you some suggestions for really deep relaxation and then guide you out of the trance state. By listening every day for one month, your experience of trance will get better and deeper with every listening.

When you experience a beautiful trance state, you'll be better able to communicate that to your clients. They will feel more confident knowing that you have experienced the hypnotic state regularly. As a result, you'll have more success in hypnotizing people simply because you know how lovely the experience is. You'll feel as if this is a gift you are sharing with them.

To avail of this fabulous free offer, all you've got to do is go to my website

www.pauljhunter.com

On the home page, scroll down a bit until you see the **FREE GIFT** section. Now just enter your name and email address and I'll email it to you immediately.

Chapter One

What Is Hypnosis?

Learning Outcomes From This Chapter
- You'll learn what the experts define hypnosis as.
- I give you my own description of hypnosis from the perspective of a practicing hypnotherapist
- You'll find out if you've ever experienced hypnosis before
- You'll learn some common examples of hypnosis from everyday life
- And finally, (and quite importantly), you'll learn what hypnosis isn't.

There are numerous definitions of hypnosis and I've outlined some of them below.

Here are some of the more famous descriptions of hypnosis -

"Hypnosis is simply exaggerated suggestibility".
George H. Estabrooks
(George Estabrooks was a prominent U.S. Psychologist who had a particular interest in military applications of hypnosis).

"A state of intensified attention and receptiveness, and an increased responsiveness to an idea or set of ideas". **Milton H. Erickson**
(Milton Erickson, 1901-1980, a psychiatrist specialising in family therapy and medical hypnosis – known as the father of modern hypnotherapy)

"Hypnosis is a state of mind in which the critical faculty of the human is bypassed, and selective thinking established". **Dave Elman**
(Dave Elman, 1900-1967, famed for his method of induction which is one of the most popular inductions taught to budding hypnotherapists).

My Own Definition Of Hypnosis
My own definition would go something like this -
"Hypnosis is a deeply relaxed state where the conscious mind becomes distracted and absorbed to a level where suggestions that are consistent with the hypnotised subjects values and beliefs become easily assimilated and as a result, rapid change is possible".

In my opinion, each of the famous hypnotherapists quoted above has defined hypnosis based upon their own experiences with their clients. So who is right? The answer is – they all are. Whatever definition you subscribe to, the important thing to remember is that a person in hypnosis can learn very easily, in both a good way and a bad way.

So, for instance, a skilled hypnotherapist can help a person with severe panic attacks to completely overcome them. However, it is also possible that a hypnotist who is untrained or inexperienced can trigger a panic attack in the same person by inadvertently using words or descriptions that trigger the person's anxiety.

A good example of this would be the case of the person with a severe fear of water who went to see a stage hypnosis show one night and ended up on stage as part of the show. This person's fear was triggered inadvertently by the hypnotist's suggestion that the person was in a dinghy out in the middle of the ocean and had to row as fast as they could to get close to a passing ship that could rescue them. For obvious reasons this triggered a severe state of fear in the person and they had rather an uncomfortable couple of hours afterwards.

Have You Ever Been In Hypnosis?

If you've never been to a hypnotherapist or have never been up on stage with a stage hypnotist you'll probably answer "No" to that question but actually the opposite is true. Most people have been in hypnosis at some stage in their lives and as a matter of fact, you probably experience hypnosis quite regularly but just don't know it.

Here are a couple of common examples of trance-like states that happened to me that you may identify with personally also -

Driving – I remember one day driving from my home in Cork (Ireland) to Galway, a trip of a couple of hundred miles. For most of the journey, I had the radio on in the background, but my mind was miles away, imagining being interviewed on radio about the launch of my first book. When I actually got to Galway, I got out of the car and someone asked me what road I had travelled. I remember looking at them blankly and saying "Em....., I don't know" and suddenly realising that the entire journey was a bit of a blank. I was so busy with my internal thoughts that I wasn't even aware of driving.

At School - It was a really warm day in early May. I was about 16 years old, hearing the droning, monotonous voice of the teacher fading into the background as I zoned out and stared out the window, thinking about that girl I was into who was just about to get off the bus at the bus stop right outside that window. My "trance" was ended rather abruptly when the teacher yelled my name and jolted me back to reality.

Watching TV - I was watching the movie "Top Gun" on TV and being so absorbed in the scene as Tom Cruise is flying the fighter jet that I just felt like I was there in the plane with him. Someone was asking me if I wanted a cup of tea and had to ask me four times in a row because I just didn't hear because I was busy flying a fighter jet.

You probably have many examples of trance-like states yourself during your daily life. Human beings have a natural ability to drift in and out of trance-like states frequently during each day.

Because it is such a natural state, when people go into hypnosis, they can sometimes say afterwards that they didn't feel hypnotized. The funny thing is that they don't actually know what being hypnotized "should" feel like. Because we experience trance-like states so regularly, hypnosis will probably just feel very natural and deeply relaxing for most people.

What Hypnosis Isn't
Hypnosis is <u>not</u> magic – some people have unrealistic expectations of what can be achieved with hypnosis. Probably an important thing to bear in mind is that you must want to change – I regard hypnosis a a method of enhancing your options, not changing your mind.

Hypnosis is <u>not</u> mind-control – hypnosis has been wrongly associated in some people's minds with mind-control or brainwashing and I often hear my clients, when they come to see me first, saying that they are a bit wary of letting someone have control of their mind. I normally have a joke with them about that, telling them that I have enough of a task controlling my own mind at times and that I haven't the slightest interest in controlling theirs.

Hypnosis is <u>not</u> dangerous – many people have this strange idea that they might get stuck in hypnosis and not be able to come out of trance. The very worst thing that could possibly happen would be that the subject would drift into a normal, natural sleep. How bad is that?

Hypnosis is <u>not</u> amnesia – many people expect that they won't remember anything afterwards and then they end up feeling they weren't hypnotised because they heard everything. This is just a misunderstanding and challenges the hypnotist to explain hypnosis better before inducing hypnosis.

Hypnosis is <u>not</u> a trippy, drugged type of state – many people expect, or even fear that it will feel weird or wonderful and ironically can be disappointed when it doesn't feel like a trippy, out-of-control experience.

So, What Have You Learned?

I'm going to pose you some questions at this point just to see what you've learned from this chapter. Whether you can answer or not should tell you whether you need to re-read this chapter or not.

1. What was the name of the psychiatrist often referred to as the father of modern hypnosis?
2. Is it possible for a hypnotist to trigger a panic attack in a client?
3. Hypothetically speaking, could you make someone steal a car using hypnosis?

Eager To Get Started?
At this stage, you are probably chomping at the bit, full of eagerness to get started and put your first subject successfully into hypnosis. I know when I started learning about hypnosis, I certainly felt like that. Don't worry, you'll be really good at it as long as you take the time to learn the basics.

This book was not written to the standards of academia on purpose. There is very little referencing or scientific language used. I prefer to leave that to others. My aim to to provide you with a comprehensive yet simple to understand set of skills that will help you to hypnotize – simple as that!

If you decide that you want to take your studies of hypnosis and hypnotherapy further, you'll come across plenty of technically written books like that, but for now, you don't really need any of that.

So if you're starting to become really excited about learning hypnosis........read on!

Chapter Two

A Brief History Of Hypnosis

Learning Outcomes From This Chapter
- You'll learn about the earliest roots of hypnosis
- You'll learn how the nature of the hypnotic trance was discovered
- You'll discover how hypnosis became integrated into therapy

There are many books that go into great detail about the history of hypnosis. For the purposes of this book which is to teach you how to hypnotize, it is not necessary to go through the entire history of hypnosis.

I do think it is important though to appreciate where hypnosis came from so that you realise that there is more to hypnosis than just stage shows. I have included some very brief references to the people who I personally regard as being important in the development of hypnosis as a therapeutic tool.

So, if you're ready for your brief but entertaining history lesson, then let's begin......!!

There was a very wise old quotation which tells us that we must know where we came from in order to understand where we are going. So I hope you'll indulge me for a short while in order to discover the rather fascinating roots of hypnosis.

4000 Years Ago

It is believed that the ancient Egyptians used what they called "Sleep Temples" to heal both mental and physical problems. The person with the problem was put into a sleep-like state during which the priests and priestesses of the sleep temple interpreted their dreams and gave them appropriate suggestions with the intention of healing their ills. You may have heard of the Egyptian high priest Imhotep, who was regarded as the most celebrated physician of the time.

There is also evidence in manuscripts from ancient India that healing trances were commonly used by the ancient Hindu's and also in ancient Greece where the Asclepian people practiced this form of healing.

I have to say when I read this, I found it rather funny. In our age of complex technology, we have a tendency to look back in time and regard ancient civilisations as being primitive or unintelligent, and yet here is a very clear example of a practice that very clearly resembles modern hypnosis in many ways. Obviously, we have refined the process significantly since then, but even in that brief description of it, you can recognise the similarities.

1700's

The next interesting phase of the development of hypnosis was in the 1700's in the person of Franz Anton Mesmer. I'm sure you've probably heard the word "mesmerized" used in everyday language – that's all due to Mr. Mesmer. He lived 1734 to 1815 and was extremely famous at the time for his theory of Animal Magnetism.

The use of magnets was not new – it had been used since the 1500's. The healer used to pass magnets over the affected area of the body or mind. Proponents of the use of magnets believed it was the magnets that cured the client. Mesmer, however, believed that the magnets just simply interacted with a natural magnetism inside the patients own body and the the cure came from inside the patient. He believed that every living thing had a sort of "cosmic fluid" flowing within them that could be influenced by magnets. Mesmer was eventually discredited because this so-called magnetism could not be measured by any expert and it was eventually concluded that he was a fraud.

It may seem funny, or almost ridiculous to us that people believed that, however, we should not discount it so lightly, because Mesmer did actually cure many thousands of people in this way. And that may prompt the question in your mind - "how did such a quack-sounding theory ever actually produce results?"

The answer, I believe, lies in what the process was described as – it was called "mesmerism". Mesmer's clients were often in a trance-like state because of Mesmer suggesting to them that they focus on the positive healing that was occurring as he was passing the magnets over their bodies. He was creating an expectancy that they were going to be cured and guess what happened in many cases – they were!

Isn't that just the placebo effect? Well let's not diss the placebo effect too quickly! The human body has powerful inbuilt programs in the subconscious mind to heal ourselves. Perhaps Mesmer was unwittingly activating those programs by the use of suggestion. And anyway, I'm sure those people that he healed didn't really give a toss how they were healed – I would guess that they were just happy to be cured!

1800's

The term "hypnosis" that we commonly use today was first coined by a young surgeon called James Braid. He went to see a demonstration of mesmerism and rather than being wowed by what was happening in front of him, he decided to observe every closely the reactions of the patient. He became convinced that the patient was focussing or staring at the mesmerist and he observed that, because of this level of absorbed attention, the patient seemed to be in a trance-like state.

As a result of his observations, he wrote a book called "Neurypnology" which was published in 1843 in which he referred to this trance-like state as neuro-hypnosis. And so the term hypnosis was born!

Exciting things were beginning to happen in the field of hypnosis because another surgeon called James Esdaile had begun using hypnosis while performing surgery on patients in India as a form of anesthetic. It seems quite difficult for us in the 21st century to grasp that there was a time when there was no such thing as general anesthetic. Imagine having some form of invasive surgery which required the surgeon to cut into your flesh or even amputate a limb. Now imagine that without general anesthetic!

The rather interesting thing that Esdaile discovered was that many patients with whom he used hypnosis recovered in less than the normal recovery time. Rather unfortunately however, chemical pain control in the form of chloroform was discovered around the same time which meant that hypnosis became redundant rather quickly.

Towards the latter end of the 1800's, another notable name to use hypnosis for a while was Sigmund Freud. When he initially began his practice, he extensively used hypnosis in his treatment of those with neurotic ailments.

He apparently stopped using hypnosis when a lady who had been in hypnosis emerged from trance and kissed him. We may only speculate exactly what his reason was for discontinuing the use of hypnosis but perhaps one explanation of it may be that he could not cope with the unexpectedly sensual nature of the lady's' reaction and didn't want to risk another similar incident.

I suppose when we read about that today, it is easy to think "Big deal – so a woman kissed him!". However, when you think back to the period in which Freud lived, there could have been a hint of scandal potentially attaching to his work if this became commonplace.

Perhaps he also could have found himself to be discredited by the scientific community at large. There was probably a great deal at risk because of this incident, so it was probably no wonder that he did the "honorable" thing at the time and ditched hypnosis.

20th Century
In the early part of the 20th century, Joseph Jastrow ran a course in the University of Wisconsin on the medical uses of hypnosis. One of his students, Clark Hull researched hypnosis at a scientific level and used modern experimental techniques as used in psychology.

From the 1960's on is generally regarded as a golden age for hypnosis. One of the most influential figures of that time was Dave Elman who will be referred to later in this book. He adapted some of the techniques used by stage performers for use in the therapeutic field and the most famous is probably what is known as the Elman Induction which is a rapid way of inducing trance. Up until this, getting a client into hypnosis had been a long and laborious process and some have described it as "boring a person into trance".

Therapist Stephen Wolinsky in his book "Trances People Live" described how modern brain imaging can show how deep trance phenomena can be found in the waking state (in other words, when you are fully conscious). He claims that there are layers of hypnotic trance that we naturally move in and out of during the course of the normal day, without even being aware of it.

And then we come to probably the most famous hypnotherapist of all – Milton Erickson. Erickson became famous for his use of metaphor in therapy - in other words, he told his clients stories that involved a character or scene that paralleled the clients problem in some way, but in which there was a good outcome.

He also has been hugely influential on modern hypnosis for his ability to utilise anything the client said or did in order to guide them into hypnosis. We'll discover more of that later in the book as you learn how to guide a person into hypnosis.

21st Century
Probably one of the most influential figures in the field of hypnosis right now is Richard Bandler. In collaboration with John Grinder, he developed the whole area of NLP (Neuro-Linguistic Programming) by carefully observing therapists such as Milton Erickson.

Bandler concentrated some of his work in the area of sub-modalities – those are the subtle distinctions that we make within each of our senses. For instance, we have a sense of sight, but when we see something, it's either near or far away, full of colour or back and white, etc, etc. NLP teaches us how to use this knowledge to change an unwanted feeling.

I would wholeheartedly recommend that, once you have perfected the techniques in this book, you read some more about NLP. You'll find some suggestions as regards which books to consider reading at the end of this book in the "Bibliography" section.

So, What Have You Learned?
Lets just see if you were paying attention during the history lesson. If you get any of these question wrong, maybe you need to re-read the chapter.
1. The ancient Japanese cultures had "Sleep Temples". True or False?
2. What type of fluid did Franz Anton Mesmer believe that human beings had flowing through them?
3. Describe how Milton Erickson used metaphor in therapy.

So, have you had enough history? Want to get on with the good stuff? Well first up, you have to learn about safety. Why? Because when you hypnotize another person, you really have a lot of responsibility to do it right so that the hypnotic trance is safe for your subject.

So if you're ready.....read on!

Chapter Three

Hypnotizing Others – Doing It Safely!

<u>Learning Outcomes From This Chapter</u>
- You'll learn about what types of people should not be hypnotised
- You'll learn about unintentionally triggering abreactions (emotional outbursts)
- You'll learn about medical issues that impact hypnosis
- You'll learn about hidden memories

The most important thing to bear in mind when hypnotizing anyone is that their safety must be of paramount importance. No matter how eager you are to prove you are a wonderful hypnotist, never lose sight of that! In order to make absolutely sure that you are acting in the best interests of your subject, it really is important to take time to consider the issues that this chapter raises.

Are There Some People Who Should Not Be Hypnotized?

YES! And it is your responsibility to know who they are. Here is a short list of those who should not be hypnotized (this is a guideline only – not an exhaustive list)
- People who suffer from epilepsy
- People who have had psychotic episodes
- People with MPD (Multiple Personality Disorder)
- People who suffer from low blood pressure.
- People who have unrealistic expectations
- People with any anxiety-related medical condition

It would probably be fair for you to ask me "But Paul, how can I be expected to know this stuff about the person I am hypnotizing?" And there is a very simple answer – ASK! It is not their responsibility to tell you – you're supposed to know this stuff if you are going to hypnotise them!

Remember the famous saying from the film Spiderman - "with great power comes great responsibility"

Lets examine each one of these in greater detail – first of all, a person with epilepsy could have an epileptic fit while in hypnosis, so it's rather obvious that would be dangerous. People with a detached sense of reality such as those who are or previously have suffered from psychotic episodes or MPD can have their conditions worsened by hypnosis unless under the supervision of a psychiatrist – in other words, don't go there!

Low blood pressure is an interesting one – hypnosis can have a side effect of lowering the blood pressure which could be dangerous for a person who already has low blood pressure. This can also prevent a person from going into trance if they notice that, as they relax, they are feeling faint.

Some people have unrealistic expectations of hypnosis, like as if it some kind of magic where you click your fingers and suddenly their phobia or traumatic memory is gone. Once again, just stick to the basics until you know more, and don't be tempted to venture where you are not qualified.

What Happens If They Didn't Tell me?

All we can do is our best. For instance, if you ask a person if they have ever had epilepsy and they answer "no". Just for this example, lets say that they haven't suffered from epilepsy in years and they are eager to experience hypnosis, so they've said no in case you refuse to hypnotize them. Then in hypnosis, they have a mild epileptic fit. What do you do? I would always say – put your clients safely first. If you are not experienced in how to help someone with an epileptic fit (most of us aren't, including me), then call 911 if the situation warrants it.

This is why explaining hypnosis to your clients is extremely important. I would always openly tell clients that hypnosis can be dangerous for those people who shouldn't be hypnotized. Then I tell them to be 100% truthful with me so I can make sure their experience of hypnosis is safe.

The great news is that it is an extremely rare occurrence that a client will lie to you or cover up something like that. I always use the mantra "if in any doubt, don't hypnotize".

What Happens If I Unintentionally Trigger An Abreaction?

First of all, what is an abreaction. Probably the best way to describe an abreaction is a sudden release of repressed emotion. I always find the best way to describe this is by using examples.

Example 1 – With a particular client of mine, I used a slightly more authoritarian tone of voice at a certain stage of the hypnosis induction and he immediately started to cry. The sudden, unexpected authoritarian tone of my voice triggered a memory of his childhood when he was being frightened by an adult's loud voice.

Example 2 – I heard this story from a colleague of mine who told me that she was guiding her client into hypnosis when she used the phrase "relax now and give yourself permission to release all that tension". Her client immediately abreacted by starting to cry. She found out later that it was the word "release" that had triggered the emotional reaction. Apparently the client had been held down at one stage and was threatened with serious consequences if she screamed when her captor "released" his grip.

In both of these cases, the reactions were triggered inadvertently – in other words, the hypnotherapist had no inkling that they were about to trigger an abreaction. And I can speak from personal experience and tell you that when that happens to you for the first time, it's a bit scary!

However, all you have to do is remain in control. Remain calm and treat the emotional outburst as if it's perfectly natural. Perhaps just soothingly say **"that's right – you can just let it all out now as the sound of my voice helps you to return to a feeling of safety here today as soon as you are ready"**.

You could also perhaps suggest to the client that they **"breathe it away"**, or **"breathe it back to the person who deserves it"**

At this point, do not try to counsel the client or attempt to get them to release any more emotion. If you do, you are straying into an area that only qualified and experienced therapists should go. As soon as the client has stopped abreacting, give some more suggestions for safety and security and terminate the trance.

I would suggest that you recommend to the person that they go see someone qualified to help them to release their emotions safely and explain that you are not qualified to go any further. Remember, by taking a chance and trying to do more than you are qualified to do, you can do untold damage.

Medical Issues That Impact Hypnosis
There are medical issues that need to be taken into account when hypnotising someone. The most obvious one's – those people who should not be hypnotised – have been discussed earlier in this chapter but now I want to tell you about some other issues of a medical nature that you need to be careful about.

First of all, with all of your wonderful new knowledge of hypnosis that you'll have by the end of this book, you may be tempted to try hypnotising a person who has a headache to see if you can "suggest" away their headache. And you may be amazed to find that you possibly could achieve that outcome.

Your hypnotic subject will probably be delighted with you and amazed at your "power" to take away pain. And you'd probably finish that session of hypnosis feeling rather proud of yourself.

Imagine, though, how you would feel if you heard the news a couple of weeks later that the person had died of a brain tumour that might have been discovered earlier if some well-meaning amateur hypnotist hadn't attempted to show off.

I know I'm being a bit harsh here but it is really important that you begin to realise that hypnosis is not just fun – it is powerful and you need to treat it with respect.

As a general rule of thumb, check with your hypnotic subject to make sure there is no medical issue in the background, there is no significant trauma from earlier in their life and most importantly, that there is no fear of anything that they can tell you about. If in doubt, always ask! And if you have any reason to wonder if hypnosis is safe to do with any individual, err on the safe side and don't do it.

The best question I ever learned to ask with my clients comes at the end of asking them lots of questions about their fears, any medical problems they had, etc. That question is - **"So, is there anything else that I should have asked you that might be relevant?"**

So What Are Hidden Memories
Hidden memories are the ability our mind has to protect us from situations that might be overwhelming to us at the time. This is why people who have, for instance, been in a horrific car crash might not be able to recall it fully. Or why a person who has suffered abuse may not be able to recall the actual event or certain parts of it.

This is a protection mechanism that is hard-wired into our brains called repression. Our mind will repress certain things about an overwhelming situation and only allow us to deal with the bits that we have the resources to deal with at that time.

The thing with hidden or repressed memories is that those negative emotions attached to those experiences are still there, under the surface, bubbling away, causing us problems in our present day life.

This is why the person who experiences an adult bullying them when they are just young can have a knot in their stomach at the time which can possibly develop into irritable bowel syndrome in later life. Now, as an adult, they may be blissfully unaware of the original incident that kicked off that tight uncomfortable feeling in their stomach, however, the symptoms will remain for as long as the original unresolved emotion remains bottled up.

It is not necessary for you to know much more than that for the purposes of learning how to hypnotize but it is important to just have an appreciation of what hidden memories are. And once again, do not be tempted to wander into territory that is outside of your ability.

Recovering hidden memories is something that requires skill and training and because you are not at that skill level, stay away from the whole area of hidden memories, and if your subject wants to uncover hidden memories, find a qualified hypnotherapist nearby who is best placed to help them.

So, What Have You Learned?
We've covered quite a bit in this chapter. Because this is really important material. if you get one of these questions wrong, please go back and learn the correct answer. Learning the correct answer could be the difference between hypnotizing someone safely, or putting them in danger.
    1. Is it ok to hypnotize someone who has suffered from psychosis, either now or at any stage in the past?

2. How would you hypnotize someone who complained of headaches?
3. What is the sentence you would say to someone who suddenly bursts into tears while under hypnosis?

So, enough of the cautions, it's time to learn how to hypnotize.......

Chapter Four

First Things First –
Learning Rapport

Learning Outcomes From This Chapter
- You'll learn the percentage of human communication that's non-verbal
- You'll learn about the importance of eye-contact
- You'll be able to list all of the main representational systems
- You'll become proficient at matching and mirroring

Rapport is vitally important to being able to hypnotize someone successfully. Take your time to practice all of the techniques you'll find in this chapter and they will reward you by helping you to become really good at hypnotising people.

Don't worry if you're a bit shy or awkward with some of these techniques at first. Let me tell you a secret – every successful hypnotist or hypnotherapist was just as awkward with these when they learned them! All you need to do is just persist with them. Practice makes perfect. The great thing about practicing rapport is that you can do it in your daily life without anyone being the wiser.

93%
Keep that figure in mind always. Especially when you are having a disagreement with your partner or with a work colleague. It'll help you to understand human communication a whole lot better.

93% is the amount of human communication that's non-verbal. Let me put that another way - what you say doesn't really matter as much as you've always thought it did! When I first heard that figure I thought - "no, that couldn't be right!"

I remember being in a boardroom of the company I used to work for (before I became a hypnotherapist) and we were having an NLP Sales Training day with a qualified NLP trainer. And he could see that none of us could quite get our heads around this idea that 93% of human communication was non-verbal. So he decided to do a little experiment with two volunteers to demonstrate. You can guess who one of the volunteers was!

He asked me to do the talking and the other guy to do the listening. He asked me to speak about something I was really passionate about which for me was my favourite soccer team Manchester United. And he asked the guy that was doing the listening to really enthusiastically listen, keeping eye contact and nodding his head, etc.

Then after a minute, the listener was supposed to turn away, break eye contact and say "keep on going – I'm still listening" with his back now turned to me. Immediately, it was as if all of the words had just fallen out of my head. I couldn't think of what to say next, I went completely blank, and more than that, I actually felt like someone had just punched me in the solar plexus and winded me.

And I invite you to try the same experiment. Here's how you do it -

Practice Exercise 1 – Non-verbal Communication
Find a friend who is willing to do this experiment with you. You can take it in turns to be the speaker and the listener so that each of you appreciates fully what non-verbal communication is. Sitting down is probably the best way to do this, with both chairs facing each other.

The speaker must find some topic that they are passionate about, something that is close to their heart, something they can get a bit emotional about as they are describing it. That could be a favourite sport or pastime, a political cause, a religious belief.....it's your choice.

The listener must position themselves straight across from the speaker and listen really enthusiastically, keeping eye contact, nodding along as if in agreement, etc.

After one minute has elapsed, the listener, should break eye contact, get up from their seat and turn their back to the speaker, breaking all non-verbal communication while saying "go on.....I'm listening."

If the speaker is in mid-flow, telling their story enthusiastically, they should notice a change in their ability to think or concentrate, they may feel a bit winded or confused.

The Power Of Eye Contact
Eye contact is a very important pre-requisite for a hypnotist. Have you ever been in conversation with someone who can't keep eye contact with you? Does it

irritate you? Does it make you wary of them? Do you distrust them, even if only slightly?

If you consider that when a person goes into hypnosis in the company of a hypnotist, in that split second as they go into hypnosis, they are essentially placing their trust in you. Remember the non-verbal communication exercise? If you can't look your client in the eye, then what does your client subconsciously pick up from that? How about - "is he sure of what he's doing?", or "do I really trust him?"

So if you're not used to making good eye contact with people, now is the time to start. With some practice, you'll be able to do what I am now able to do – that is, to look a person in the eye while detaching your thought process so that you can internally observe the other persons' slightest changes in expression, blink rate, eye movements etc while still being able to maintain a conversation with that person.

Once again, remember non-verbal communication! Wouldn't it be wonderful if you didn't even have to say a word but could still induce hypnosis in a person? Well learning eye contact is an important part of being able to do that, so don't skip it. Take your time to do the exercise below.

I remember being taught about eye contact as a twenty two year old by an NLP (Neuro-Linguistic Programming) trainer who suggested that when I was on a train that evening that I should initiate eye contact with a female on the other train that was in the same station at the same time. (In order to avoid a possible relationship breakup, I'd like to point out that this was long before I'd met the love of my life!).

He suggested that I keep eye contact with the person for five seconds longer than seemed comfortable and to then look away. I was to count to five and then look back again and see if the girl was still staring at me. She was! And she gave me a nice smile into the bargain, which gave me a fair degree of amusement but also gave me a powerful lesson in the power of eye contact.

Practical Exercise 2 – Establishing powerful eye contact

In a social or family situation, when you are having a conversation with someone, start to become a bit more aware of eye contact. There is no need to inform the other person in advance or pre-warn them.

Start off by keeping eye contact throughout the conversation. At any time that you are tempted to look away, resist the temptation, and continue looking into the other persons eyes as if you're completely absorbed in what they are saying. Notice how your enjoyment of the conversation increases when you are non-verbally communicating better.

When you have achieved maintaining eye contact regularly, now begin to notice things about the other person. What are they doing with their eyes as they speak? Are they moving up, sideways, down or are they looking away at times? Notice how often their eyelids blink. Notice if their eyelids have a little "double flutter" at times.

Now notice the rate at which they are blinking and match your rate of blinking to theirs. After a while (about a minute or two), change the rate of your blinking and notice if they follow you and change their blink rate also. You'll learn more about this in the following sections on Matching and Mirroring

Main Representational Systems

We all have five senses – sight, hearing, touch, smell and taste. That's how we interpret the outside world. And we all use one of those senses perhaps a bit more than the others. The main three representational systems tend to be Visual, Auditory or Kinaesthetic and I'll explain what those mean so that you'll understand easily.

If a person's main representational system is Visual, it will be noticeable that they'll express themselves by using some of the following - "that looks good to me", "I get the picture", "I see what you mean", etc. In other words, the words or phrases that they use to describe things or situations are primarily visual as in the examples above.

If the persons primary representational system is auditory, then they may use phrases such as "I hear what your saying", "that sounds good to me", etc.

If a persons primary representational system is kinaesthetic, the may talk about experiences or feelings, for example "I don't get a good feeling about that", or "that feels right to me", etc.

Now the thing with representational systems is that we can find ourselves using all of the above statements from time to time. When I talk about <u>primary</u> representational system, what is actually meant is the one we tend to use the most. That does not mean we necessarily exclude all other representational systems – it just means that we use one more than the others.

And in terms of identifying which representational system a person uses most, that just requires you to become more observant. You'll become very good at this if you persist with it and the best way to practice is to do it covertly – in other words observe your partner, your brother, your girlfriend, your work colleague, your friend, or whatever person that you interact with regularly.

Practical Exercise 3 - Identifying Representational Systems

Begin by becoming more observant of people around you. Listen to what they are saying when they communicate. What are the words they use a lot to describe things?

When you observe some people, you'll find it's immediately obvious that they are primarily visual, and then with others, it's more difficult to ascertain. These are the interesting ones! As you get better and better at this, you'll find yourself beginning to identify more and more primary representational systems. Don't worry though – even I don't identify them in everyone every time.

Now I'd like you to begin to use whatever is that persons primary representational system in your communication with them. In other words, if they are auditory, begin to use phrases such as "that sounds good to me", etc and notice how your communication with that person seems to improve.

Many communication problems within families, between teacher and pupil or between work colleagues lies in the fact that, for example, one person is primarily visual and the other is kinaesthetic – in essence, it's like we're talking in different languages.

What Is Matching And Mirroring?

Put quite simply, this is when we copy the other persons body language or vocal patterns. There are plenty of examples of this in real life where people are blissfully unaware that they're doing this.

Take for example a couple who are in a bar or restaurant together and are obviously madly in love. If you observe them closely, it's quite likely that you'll spot that they are making wonderful eye contact. They are probably doing the same things with their bodies such as crossing their legs in the same way, or doing the same things with their hands.

When you become an avid observer of people, you'll begin to notice patterns emerging. You'll notice that those who have the best relationships are doing a whole load of things at a non-verbal level that are similar to each other. And of course when another person is doing the same as you are, unconsciously you are beginning to think that they are just like you so they must be nice, and you may feel very comfortable in their company.

I told you a story earlier about eye contact where the NLP trainer that was giving a sales course suggested that we put our newfound knowledge of NLP into practice in our personal lives. He suggested we did the same with matching and mirroring.

A colleague of mine at the time decided to put his new matching and mirroring knowledge into practice with a receptionist in the company we were both working for at the time. He decided that every day for the following week, he was going to make really good eye contact with this lady and match and mirror her body movements as she was speaking to him.

Now he'd been working in this company for about three years and this lady had never taken much notice of him. Within one week, not only were they communicating much better than before, on the Friday evening she actually asked him out on a date. He told me afterwards that if he was sceptical about this stuff as we were learning it on the day, he was a convert by the end of that week.

So, how can you use this to your advantage? Well the following Practical Exercise will help you to practice matching and mirroring

Practical Exercise 4 – Matching & Mirroring

Pick someone who is close to you (eg, your wife, girlfriend, boyfriend, etc) and notice their body movements. Notice what they are doing with their hands (are they clasped together, are they gesturing, etc?). Also, notice what they are doing with their legs (crossed or not). The notice their breathing – is it fast or slow? Notice their eyes and how fast they blink. Notice the tone of their voice, the pace of their voice, the words they use, etc.

Now gradually and without causing the person to notice what you are doing, begin to match their hands, their legs, their breathing, their tone of voice, etc. Match as many things about them as you can, doing exactly what they are doing. Notice what happens – does the quality of your communication with the person seem to be better?

Now mirror their actions. Mirroring is doing the mirror image of what they are doing. In other words, imagine you are a mirror – if the person raises their right hand, you would need to raise your left hand in order to correctly mirror them.

It'll be fascinating to notice how the quality of your communication gets so much better as you do as I've suggested above.

So, What Have You Learned?

Here are some questions to test whether you retained the information you read earlier in this chapter.

1. What percentage of human communication is non-verbal?
2. What are the names of the three main representational systems?
3. What is matching and mirroring?

Well done on your learning so far. It's important to remember that you won't remember everything in your first read of this book. I recommend going back over it again in a couple of weeks and becoming aware of how much you retained from the first reading of the book. When you study this book for a second time, you will retain more. If you intend to pursue a career as a hypnotherapist, I would strongly recommend reading this book many times until you know every part of it by heart.

Now then, onwards to suggestibility tests.

Chapter Five

Suggestibility Tests

<u>Learning Outcomes From This Chapter</u>
- You'll be able to explain what a suggestibility test actually is
- You'll learn why we need to do suggestibility tests
- You'll learn what to look for during a suggestibility test
- You'll learn three simple suggestibility tests
- You'll learn about repeating suggestibility tests until you get the desired results

What Is A Suggestibility Test?

In order to answer that question, we need to understand what suggestibility actually is. Whenever I mention "suggestibility" to my clients, some of them think being suggestible is a bad thing. It might mean they are gullible, easily led, or a bit stupid. One of the first things I have to explain is that suggestibility is the very basis of how we learn. Consider some of these examples -

Example No. 1 – When you are a baby, your mother showed you how to use a spoon to feed yourself. She was suggesting that you follow her actions and you did, and that's why you can now feed yourself. So, that's good, right?

Example No.2 – When you were at school for the first time, your teacher suggested things like perhaps the picture of a cat for the letter "c" and that's how you began to learn your alphabet. So, essentially, your teacher suggested something to you, and you learned language as a result. So if you didn't follow the teachers suggestions, you wouldn't be able to read or write or do all those other things that school taught you.

Suggestibility is just about our ability to learn – that's all.

So why is it important in the area of hypnosis? Well even though every human being experiences a form of hypnosis during their everyday lives, they just don't know that it's hypnosis.

So when you come along to hypnotise them, they can think that this is something that they've never experienced before. As a result, they feel as if they do not know how to do this thing called hypnosis which can cause them to be a bit anxious or feel as if they have to make some form of effort in order to go into hypnosis. It is this very effort that may cause them difficulty in achieving a satisfactory level of hypnosis.

Because hypnosis is similar to sleep, it is easy to understand that you don't make an effort to go to sleep – it just kind of happen, doesn't it? And it's the same with hypnosis – you just have to allow it to happen.

Your role is to teach your client how to let go, how to do nothing and how to trust you and follow your instructions. When I do a suggestibility test with a client, the reason that I want to client to be able to do what

I suggest is because I want the client to follow my instructions without necessarily being consciously aware that they doing what I am suggesting.

This means that, later on, when I suggest that will go into hypnosis, relax easily and go even deeper, they will accept my suggestions without consciously analysing them or overthinking.

Three Simple Suggestibility Tests
The key to getting the most accurate results with suggestibility tests in my humble opinion is to be completely confident in your approach. The client will unconsciously pick up on your confidence and will be more likely to follow your instructions. Your voice especially should convey that confidence – you should speak confidently and authoritatively and this will create an expectation in your client, an expectation of success.

Suggestibility Test No. 1 – Imaginary String
Tell your client that they should clasp their hands together, palms nice and tight together, locking their fingers together except for their first finger of either hand which should stand upright and parallel to each other a little like football goalposts. Explain again that the palms should be nice and tight together.

Then suggest that you are about to tie some imaginary string around your clients fingers. Actually touch your clients upright fingers with one of yours as you pretend to tie that string around their fingers. Then suggest that right next to the clients fingers, there is a sort of turnscrew which will tighten the imaginary string.

Pretend to turn this turnscrew with your fingers while you say the following - "Now I'm not too sure if you can feel the string beginning to tighten right now or perhaps you'll just notice that it seems as if your fingers are just being attracted towards each other now as I tighten that turnscrew and that string draws your fingers even closer together until they touch".

At any stage at which your client seems to be obeying your instructions, always say "that's right". This will reinforce the clients willingness to follow your instructions.

One of three things will happen –
1. *they will follow your instructions and probably start laughing at how they have no control over their own fingers. You have succeeded and unconsciously, they have learned how to follow your instructions;*
2. *their fingers will not move towards each other and this tells you that either they are resisting your instructions or else they are quite analytical and logical in their thinking or*
3. *they will do the exact opposite of what you are suggesting in which case, there may be some anxiety or fear of hypnosis, or they may misunderstand what's going on, or they may just be analytical.*

Whichever happens, this is all good. It just gives you information as to how to proceed.

In the case of (1), you know your client is following your instructions so you could proceed immediately to hypnotizing them, or you could do another suggestibility test to be doubly sure that they are following your every instruction. If you decide to go ahead and hypnotize them, you can be (fairly) sure they will follow your instructions and will go into hypnosis.

In the case of (2), you may need to repeat the suggestibility test until they unconsciously "get" what it is you want them to do, or you could proceed to another suggestibility test. Alternatively, you could proceed to hypnotizing them using a confusional or overload style induction.

In the case of (3) it may be necessary to ask if the client is unsure or anxious about anything. Ask if their understanding of hypnosis is ok and reassure them again that it is perfectly safe.

Suggestibility Test No. 2 – The Sway Test

Get your client to stand with their back to you. Stand behind your client in such a way that you are ready to support their body weight. You could move one of your feet back about 24 inches to help you to support your clients weight if they fall back towards you (whatever seems comfortable to you).

Now instruct your client to move their feet together so that their feet and legs are tight together. When they do so, say "that's right, very good".

Then tell them to make a fist with their right hand and make their whole right arm stiff and rigid. Say "that's right, very good" when they are doing it. Now tell them to continue keeping their right arm stiff and rigid while now doing the same with their left arm. Praise again and then tell your client to make their entire body just as stiff and rigid as their arms already are. Praise again as they are doing it.

Now tell them that you are about to place the palms of your hands flat on their shoulder blades. Now actually do it. Hold that for a minute, continuing to say "that's right" and then tell your client that as you gently remove your hands, they will feel like falling backwards and they can can fall backwards perfectly safely because you will be there to catch them. Tell them they are falling backwards now.

The moment you see the person swaying, say "that's right, just let it happen now, falling backwards now". Praise when your client completes this task successfully and tell them that means they are suggestible and they will experience excellent hypnosis really easily.

The whole point of the Sway Test is to get your client to trust you and follow your instructions. If it has not happened as I have described above, you can say to your client "excellent, I am delighted that you have proved to yourself that you are in control. Now that you know you are in control, I'd like you to prove to yourself that you can feel like falling backwards, so lets do that again....".

Repeat the process until the client follows your instructions effortlessly and easily, without feeling that he or she is just doing it to "go along with you". In this respect, you may find with some clients that it may be more appropriate to just do this a couple of times and then move on and try another test instead.

Suggestibility Test No. 3 – Finger Spread Test
Get your client to sit straight upright, feet on the floor and palms resting on their thighs. Tell the client that there is no right way and no wrong way to do this and that the test just helps you to figure out which part of their brain is more dominant, their creative right brain or their logical left brain.

Now take one of their hands and hold the arm firmly so that their palm is facing their face, about ten inches away, and a little above their eye level, and at the same time hold their elbow with your other hand. Now, with the hand that was holding the elbow, tap their middle finger three or four times while saying "now I want you to stare intensely at your middle finger and when I let go of your hand in a moment, your fingers will begin to spread out. That's right!

Now let go of their hand completely while saying "separating now, that's right, separating, further and further apart" Allow about a minute to elapse, noticing whatever happens. If their fingers separate, the client is physically suggestible.

Now take their hand gently and return it to their thigh. Do not talk at this stage.

Now take their other hand and move it upwards to within ten inches of their face just as you did before. Keep silent during this. Tap their middle finger three or four times just as before and silently mouth the words "separating, that's right, separating further and further apart" while gently nodding your head. Allow 30 seconds to a minute to elapse as you just observe what happens. Then gently take their hand and return it to their thigh, telling the client that they have done very well.

With all suggestibility tests, there are two major components – (1) how open the client is to the test (2) how confident and polished you are. The only one of those two that you have complete control over is (2). You have to practice these tests until you can do them without thinking – that way you'll free yourself to be able to observe your client and react more naturally and easily which in turn will make your suggestibility tests more successful.

What To Look For During A Suggestibility Test

When I do a suggestibility test with a client, I always look for little hints that they are following my instructions. When I see or hear or sense even the slightest hint that they are following my instructions, I say "that's right".

This is absorbed by the persons unconscious as praise for doing the correct thing and therefore they will tend to do more of the thing that affirms that they are doing well. This is a most important thing for you to learn.

I will outline some suggestibility tests below, but the tests themselves are a bit incidental. What happens during the test is what's important. I regard them as an opportunity to teach my client exactly what I want the client to do later.

That doesn't mean I get it perfectly right all the time the first time that I do these tests by the way. Which neatly takes me to our next topic for discussion – why repeat a suggestibility test?

Why Repeat A Suggestibility Test?
Remember, the aim of a suggestibility test is not success or failure – it's about your client learning to follow your instructions. So, sometimes, if it's appropriate, I will repeat a suggestibility test until the client eventually follows my instructions.

Now sometimes I'll have a client who just doesn't follow my instructions during the suggestibility tests but yet experiences good hypnosis eventually. So if they don't quite work exactly how you think they should, don't worry. There is no failure, just feedback and it's what you do with that feedback that counts.

It's vitally important that you never criticise your client. Never, ever tell your client that what they are doing is wrong – that'll just cause them to resist you even more as every moment goes by. Keep on telling them that they are doing very well, exactly as you would expect, tell them that they will increasingly enjoy following your instructions, etc. Keep on saying "that's right" every time they do something that seems to indicate they are following your instructions.

Doing this in an encouraging but soothing tone of voice can send a small percentage of your clients immediately into trance, before you expect it. I have learned through experience to expect just about anything to happen – that way you'll always be prepared!

As you learn to relax and go with the flow and just deal with whatever happens, you'll become so relaxed and confident that your success at hypnotizing people will increase as well.

So, What Have You Learned?
Here are a couple of questions to test how well you remember the last few pages.

1. What does "suggestibility" mean?
2. Why would you use a suggestibility test with a client before hypnotizing them?
3. What would cause you to consider repeating a suggestibility test?

I strongly suggest that you practice at least one of the suggestibility tests listed above and become good at it. This will make you appear to be much more confident when leading up to leading a person into hypnosis. That brings up neatly to our next chapter all about hypnotic inductions.

Chapter Six

Hypnotic Inductions

Learning Outcomes From This Chapter
- You'll learn what a hypnotic induction is
- You'll learn what the different types of induction are
- You'll learn how to choose an induction for a particular client to suit their mindset
- You'll learn three popular inductions in differing styles
- You'll learn what to do if it doesn't work.

So, What Is A Hypnotic Induction?

A hypnotic induction is quite simply the method that you use to put a person into hypnosis. There are a number of methods that hypnotists commonly use including eye fixation, progressive relaxation, confusional methods, etc., and we will discuss some of these a little later on in this chapter.

When you first start to hypnotize people, it is handy to have a particular induction learned word for word so that you know what to do at all stages of the induction and what to say next. As you get better and better at hypnotizing people, you may completely abandon your original "learned off" induction, but for now, it's best to learn at least one induction perfectly so that you appear completely confident.

The biggest problem for many would-be hypnotists is that fear that an induction won't work and not knowing what to do next. That is success / failure thinking – you either succeed at putting someone into trance or you fail.

As you practice more and more hypnotic inductions, I would like you to start thinking more in terms of feedback instead. So instead of thinking "I've succeeded" or "I've failed", I'd like you to begin thinking that the clients reaction to your induction is just feedback that you can use to help you.

A good example would be if you were to instruct a client to close their eyes and allow their eyelids to relax so much that they just wouldn't open. When you test this and ask the client to try to open their eyes, if they can actually open their eyes and you are using success / failure thinking, the thought "Oh crap, it didn't work!" could cross your mind.

If you are using feedback thinking, you would react by saying "that's great. I'm delighted you've proved to yourself that you can open your eyes. Now I want you to prove equally as strongly that you can relax those eyelids so much that they just won't open". This is called utilisation and we'll discuss this more in Chapter Seven.

Do you understand how this is incredibly powerful? How it can help your client to go deeply into hypnosis? And how your style of thinking can influence your client to begin thinking in terms of feedback rather than success or failure also, making him / her more relaxed and more trusting of you.

What Are The Main Types Of Hypnotic Induction?

There are a number of different styles of hypnotic induction and the main one's are listed here – there's progressive relaxation induction, eye fixation inductions, fractional inductions, confusional inductions, overload inductions and rapid inductions. Now there are more inductions than these but these are enough to keep you busy for starters. At a later stage, you can go on to learn more induction types if you want. Let's discuss the types of induction listed above and learn what types of people these will work well with.

Progressive Relaxation Induction – this is a good, general purpose induction suitable for most people with a relatively good imagination who are agreeable to the idea of hypnosis and who have no hang-ups or reluctance about hypnosis. The whole idea of progressive relaxation is to concentrate all of the clients attention on different parts of their body in turn and consciously relax every muscle in their body as you suggest to them how to relax.

Eye Fixation Inductions – You simply get the client to stare at a fixed object, become completely absorbed in it and then give suggestions as to how their eyelids are becoming heavier and heavier until they close. Every blink the client gives should be acknowledged by a "that's right".

Fractional Inductions – A fractional induction is where, for instance, you could get the client to slowly open and close their eyes, each time giving a suggestion for even more heaviness in the eyelids. As the client gets used to following your instructions, when this works really well, after four or five repetitions, the client will find it really difficult to open their eyes again.

Confusional Inductions – These are used with clients who have a tendency to be very logical or analytical or who have difficulty in imagining or relaxing. The whole point is to confuse their mind so much that when the "easy" option of just relaxing is presented to them, they will take the path of least resistance and just relax.

Overload Inductions – Psychologists tell us that human beings can only take in seven plus or minus two inputs into our senses at the same time, so you can achieve trance with a client by suggesting more and more sensory inputs – for instance "perhaps you can concentrate right now on your breathing" and then "at the same time as you are concentrating on your breathing, perhaps you could also concentrate now on the sensations as you hands touch the armrests there". When you build up more and more of these sensory inputs, the client feels overloaded and then it is easy to suggest complete relaxation.

Rapid Inductions – these are the type of inductions favoured by stage hypnotists because they are quick and dramatic. If your client has control issues and doesn't like feeling out of control, this may not be the best type of induction to use. I have recently started using rapid inductions in my clinical work with overly logical and analytical clients because the induction happens so quickly, they don't have time to analyse it, but as a rule, I generally stick with some form of progressive relaxation.

How To Choose An Induction
When you are starting out hypnotizing people for the first time, it may seem a bit confusing as regards which

induction to choose. When I started, I used what is popularly called the Elman Induction (named after the famous hypnotist Dave Elman).

This is quite a simple all-purpose induction and I find it works quite well for most people. As a matter of fact, I think I used this method of induction for my first twenty of thirty clients until I relaxed a bit more with it and learned to interweave bits of one induction into another and just do what seemed natural for the client.

As I mentioned in the introduction to this book – my very first client was a medical doctor who came to me to stop smoking. Because of this, I felt extremely nervous and the thought did pass through my mind "Oh crap, he's a doctor, he's going to know that I am not very good at this and he's going to spot that I'm a complete amateur and that I'm nervous".

It took me until about 15 minutes into his session to realise "hang on a second here – he probably knows nothing at all about hypnosis.....I'm the expert here". Honestly, I look back now and am very grateful for that baptism of fire. It taught me to be very resilient and to remain calm and flexible no matter what happens, especially if I am doing a hypnotic induction and it's not working.

Even though I am a seasoned hypnotherapist and I am far better now than when I first began, there is still a client pops up every so often that throws me a curve ball or does not react the way I expect. When that happens to me now, I just flow effortlessly into another method without the client even being aware I am switching techniques.

In saying that, I am not attempting to present myself as being the world's best hypnotist – I'm probably not.

All I've done is just practiced.....and practiced.....and practiced......and kept on wondering to myself "I wonder what would happen if I did this instead of that, or if I blended this technique with that", etc.

In terms of choosing an induction to suit your client, here's what I do -

• Firstly, I closely observe the client while I am having a chat with them about their problem (if they have one), or about hypnosis at the start. I'm observing what their eye movements are telling me, what their favourite representational system is (are they visual, auditory, etc), what their thinking style is (do they seem creative & imaginative or are they rigid or very logical in their thinking).

• Secondly, I form an impression about what they feel about hypnosis – are they wary of it, are they really nervous, are they calm and ok with it or are they over-excited about it and expect too much of it.

• Thirdly, I gauge the clients reaction to the suggestibility tests. If they follow my directions perfectly, they are probably going to go into hypnosis easily and something like progressive relaxation will work very well for them. If they have difficulty doing the suggestibility tests (eg. If their fingers do not spread out in the finger spread test), then that probably means they are logical or analytical in their thinking style and it can possibly indicate that using a confusional induction may work best.

Now there is no hard and fast rule that says, once you pick out an induction for your client, that it will definitely work first time. With most people, just doing what I've outlined above is enough. There are some people (thankfully, only a small proportion of people) that still do not go into hypnosis even if you've done everything correctly up until this point.

My belief is that the key to having success with these people is to persist. Keep going. Do your induction over again. Repeat things you've said before and remain confident and in control – nothing ruins rapport better than your client sensing that you don't know what to do next.

Most of my clients (even the difficult ones) would go into hypnosis quite easily normally taking five to ten minutes to experience a nice level of hypnosis. However, I am reminded of one that I don't think I'll ever forget. It was a smoking client who worked in a very creative career (so it was easy to assume that the person had a good imagination). This client took 55 minutes to go into hypnosis. I have to admit that after about 45 minutes I did consider going out to my garden shed and getting a sledgehammer and just bashing him over the head with it.

Seriously though, he was the single most difficult client I have ever had in terms of guiding him into hypnosis. And that reminded me very clearly that no matter how much I already know, there is always more to learn. The great thing about clients like him is that they are few and far between and I sincerely hope that you do not come across one of those until you are very comfortable with hypnotizing people.

Three Hypnotic Inductions
I am going to outline for you three hypnotic inductions which will help you to begin hypnotising people. The key to becoming really good at hypnotising people is practice. If I were you, I would memorise each word of one induction to start with and then practice that. Then move on to the next one and do the same.

With each induction you learn, you'll become more comfortable and may find yourself blending sentences from one into the other. There are hundreds of possible inductions and you'll probably find one that becomes your favourite. That is the very thing you must beware of. Do not become overly reliant on one hypnotic induction just because you like it.

Remember, you're not the person going into hypnosis. You must suit the induction to the client, not to you. You may remember me using the word "flexible" earlier in this chapter. I would really recommend that you develop as much flexibility as possible in the way you induce hypnosis. That way, you are giving yourself the maximum opportunity for success every time.

Induction No.1 – Progressive Relaxation
Ok. First of all, I want you to take a nice deep breath in through your nose and out through your mouth. As you breathe in, hold the breath for the count of five and then release it slowly, that's right, pushing that breath out as far as you can, that's right, further than that.....that's right. Very good.

(If the client is not following your every command, you need to keep going at this until the client is doing exactly what you have said in the exact order in which you are saying it.)

Now take another deep breath, holding it for the count of five, and then releasing it slowly, allowing your stresses and tensions to begin to drain away as you breathe out completely.

And now finally, one last deep breath, this time as you are breathing out, I'd like you to allow your eyelids to close really slowly, little by little, that's right, just little by little, noticing how relaxed they become as you allow them to slowly close now.

(At this stage, your clients eyelids should be closed. If, for any reason, they are not, instruct you client firmly to close their eyes now.)

Now breathing slowly and easily, I want you to concentrate all of your attention on your toes, and I want you to consciously and unconsciously relax those toes now. Relax them so much that they feel wonderful. Now notice any tension, any slight tightness in of those little muscles on the soles of your feet and just loosen them and relax them now. That's right. Perhaps that relaxation in your feet can just continue to deepen now with every easy breath you take.

As your concentration smoothly drifts upwards into your lower legs, become aware now of any slight tightness or tension in those muscles and perhaps you could allow your imagination to wonder how beautifully relaxed those muscles could become if they are ten times more relaxed now.

I'm not sure what sensations you'll experience in those lower legs as they relax now and I wonder perhaps if you're beginning to really enjoy this nice sensation of deep relaxation spreading from your toes to your feet to your lower legs now.

And as you let your awareness drift upwards towards your thighs, become aware of any tension in those thigh muscles and then consciously and consciously allow them to completely relax now, perhaps feeling a lovely wave of relaxation just flowing through those muscles as you become much more relaxed now..

As your awareness continues to drift on upwards into your stomach and your chest, I wonder if you can intensify your awareness of these areas of your body now and then just relax all those muscles and sinews and tissues and fibres in your chest and your stomach and enjoy loosening and relaxing them so much now that it almost seems as if you are already in that deeply relaxed state just before you drift off to sleep every night.

Now let your awareness focus on your arms, your fingers, your wrists, your forearms and upper arms, all the way up to your shoulders and even those muscles across your collarbones and into your neck. Loosen and relax them just as before there as you hear the soothing sound of my voice that seems to relax those muscles now.

Perhaps you can feel that relaxing sensation now oozing upwards into your jaw and your face, loosening every muscle, relaxing every sinew, freeing every fibre of your being and feeling a lovely wave of relaxation flowing all the way up into your brain so that your brain itself just seems to drift and relax and feel wonderful now.

Because there's a part of you that knows just how to really let go now, that means you're in control and it feels great to be in control as you let go now. Remember, nobody wants anything, nobody needs anything and there's nothing at all for you to do except to relax now. No matter how deeply you go into hypnosis now, my voice will continue to go with you, keeping you safe and secure for as long as this trance lasts.

Induction No.2 – Confusional Induction
(Start this induction rapidly and after the second paragraph, begin to slow your pace. Your client will follow your non-verbal cue to slow down and go into trance)

As you sit here in that chair there hearing the sound of my voice trying to be aware there of the exact meaning of the words you hear here and concentrating so intensely on every sound here or every sensation there, you can continue to begin or if you prefer you can begin to continue to..... relax now.

As you relax now, you can be aware of so many things that you aren't even aware of...so very aware there and so unconcerned here. Perhaps you are listening with your conscious mind more than your unconscious mind now and then perhaps that gently changes now as your conscious mind doesn't mind drifting off into a daydream while your subconscious mind takes over for a while while your conscious mind is far away no longer bothered to listen quite as carefully as before. I wonder if you can completely trust your subconscious mind to take over now or would your prefer to wait for one minute until it takes over completely there.

Keeping your eyes closed becomes even more enjoyable now as you listen more and more with your subconscious mind and less and less with your conscious mind. It's so amusing when you think that we forget using our conscious mind but our subconscious mind never forgets and yet we try so hard using our conscious mind to remember instead of forgetting to remember consciously and remembering to trust our subconscious mind never to forget. Perhaps the trick is allowing your conscious mind not to mind what it forgets because your subconscious mind will remember what it has forgotten.

It can be amusing too to consider just how many things can seem to be one thing and then turn out to be another like one and one is two and too can also mean also and hear might mean one thing to one person there or something else to another person here depending on how they choose to hear it here, or depending on how your pronounce it armless can mean two different things too or is that also. I can say so many things that you can choose to hear or not.....here with your subconscious mind as you allow your conscious mind to sleep now. Allow you conscious mind to sleep now.....deeper and deeper....and deeper......drifting farther and farther away.

Induction No. 3 – Rapid Induction

Put you hand out, palm upwards. In an authoritative voice, say the following to the client -
"Place your hand on top of mine and press down quite hard."

When the client has done this, say
"That's great. Perfect. Just like that. Now close your eyes while you continue to press down on my hand."

Wait for a few moments until the client is really focussing on the two tasks (pressing down and keeping the eyes closed. Select your moment and really fast, whip your hand out from under the clients hand while saying "SLEEP NOW" in a very loud voice.

Immediately firmly (but gently) grasp the clients head with one hand and rock it back and forth while saying "That's right, sleep now, just go deeper, every movement of your head helping you to relax more....deeper.....much deeper.....that's right.....sleep now..."

(This induction requires a VERY rapid approach. You have to be very fast because that moment of confusion created by whipping your hand out from under the clients hand will only last very briefly and if you hesitate or are slow in your delivery, the client will emerge from trance).

What To Do If The Induction Doesn't Work

This is the nightmare of all budding hypnotists. What if it doesn't work? Will I look like a prize idiot if the clients eyes open or if they say "It's not working for me". I'd like to share with you one or two of my experiences from when I first hypnotized people.

One of the scariest moments of my hypnosis career was about thirty minutes in with a particular client. I had done my progressive relaxation induction perfectly and it had worked beautifully. I deepened and then tested and everything was going great! And then, just as I was about to begin to get the client to imagine some things, the clients eyes opened. I don't know who got a bigger shock. I know that on the inside, I could hear my own internal voice shouting "Oh s**t, what do I do now?"

I'm not really sure how I came up with what I said next. It just kind of came to me instinctually. I said
"Wow, I'm so impressed that you have so much control in hypnosis that you can even open your eyes. That's wonderful. You're really good at this. And whenever you are ready to go even deeper into a really enjoyable trance, even deeper than before then those eyelids can slide closed again but only as quickly as you can enjoy going deeper now...."

And to my eternal relief, the client did just that. I was never so relieved as when I saw the clients eyelids sliding closed again. Your first time is always a bit scary, no matter whether it's hypnotizing someone or driving a car for the first time. Now, I just go with the flow and react automatically and with ease (and I'm quite relaxed while hypnotizing people too!)

Before I even start a hypnosis session, I pre-frame – that is I tell the client that I am not here to prove that hypnosis exists and whatever the client experiences will be their unique experience. I make it clear that I am not responsible for the quality of hypnosis they experience – they are!

That way, I take all of the pressure off myself to "perform" wonderful hypnosis. Ironically, because I do that, my clients generally experience really good hypnosis because they take responsibility for it themselves.

To answer the question that this section poses "What do I do if the induction doesn't work?" - well I just try something else, switch techniques, blend in elements of other approaches or inductions. Remember it's not the induction that achieves good hypnosis – it's your client that does that, so suit what you say to the person sitting in front of you and you'll be fine.

So, What Have You Learned?
Time to test yourself. If you've answered any of these questions incorrectly, don't head on to the next chapter just yet. Hypnotic inductions are the foundation stone upon which all good hypnotic experiences are built. You really should commit every detail of this chapter to memory. It will help you immeasurably in successfully hypnotizing anyone.
1. List three types of hypnotic induction.
2. What is the type of induction that you shouldn't use with someone who doesn't like the idea of losing control?
3. What can you do if your induction doesn't work?

I can't emphasize enough how important it is for your induction to flow. It doesn't flow if you are scrambling inside your mind to try and figure out what comes next. This is why I recommend learning at least one induction by heart. Now once you've got your client starting to go into trance, it's time to go deeper.

Chapter Seven

Deepening Trance

<u>Learning Outcomes From This Chapter</u>
- You'll learn why we deepen trance
- You'll learn three simple deepening techniques
- You'll learn about testing the level of trance a client is experiencing
- You'll learn about how deep the client can go
- You'll learn what utilization is and how to use it to your benefit

So Why Do We Bother To Deepen Trance?

What you've achieved in the previous chapter is eye closure and getting the client nicely relaxed. The client at this stage is probably experiencing a nice light level of trance but may not have recognised that they are experiencing trance.

Because hypnosis is a thing that naturally happens to human beings up to one hundred and twenty times a day, a person who has not experienced hypnosis before may not realise that this is hypnosis. At this stage if they were to open their eyes and return to full awareness, they would probably say "I was deeply relaxed alright but I don't think I was hypnotized"

It is your job now to deepen the trance so much that they really know this was a special and lovely experience that they can proudly call hypnosis. From my work with clients my opinion is that some of them need to be convinced that this thing called hypnosis actually exists.

Here's an important point – it is not your job to convince them that hypnosis exists. It is your job to show them how to convince themselves. That's a subtle but important distinction!

For most work in hypnosis a light or medium state is perfectly sufficient. You can, of course carry on deepening and produce deep, somnambulistic states if you (or your client) wishes. Deepening trance allows the client to achieve a nice medium state that definitely seems different to what they may ever have experienced before which allows them to say afterwards "yep, I was definitely hypnotized" and really know that it has happened for them. After successful deepening, they are much more likely to emerge from trance and say that it was wonderful and that they had never been as deeply relaxed as that before.

In my experience, I have found that the more the client believes that they were hypnotized, the easier it will be for them to make the changes that I have suggested. This can be beneficial as a therapist if you are trying to get a person to let go of a phobia that severely limits their life.

Three Simple Deepeners

The following are three rather simple deepeners that I regularly use. As with the inductions that you would have come across in the previous chapter, when you begin first, you may decide to stick rigidly to the wording I have outlined. As time goes by, you may find yourself relaxing with it more and varying what you say to suit each client.

Deepener No. 1 – Simple Countdown

As you're sitting there continuing to relax deeper and deeper now, I'm going to count down from ten to zero in a moment. With each number I count, you'll find yourself drifting deeper and deeper into a lovely state of even deeper relaxation as you breathe deeper and easier with each number as you allow yourself permission to just let go now.

So lets begin

Ten – So nice to continue to begin to relax now

Nine – Giving yourself permission to completely let go now

Eight – What if you really enjoy the feelings within you as you go deeper now

Seven – Your breathing and heartrate slow and relaxed now

Six – Muscles loosening becoming limp and lazy as you relax even more

Five – So lovely to go even deeper now as thoughts just seem to float

Four – Feeling so calm, so peaceful in your mind and your body

Three – It just keeps getting more enjoyable the deeper you go

Two – Even deeper now....that's right.....even deeper

One – No-one needs anything ..... no-one wants anything and that means

Zero – You can completely let go now and drift down down down to your perfect level of lovely enjoyable hypnotic relaxation.....that's right

Deepener No. 2 - Wave After Wave
(Use with clients who have told you that their favourite place to relax is a beach)

As you're sitting there continuing to relax more with each easy breath you take, I wonder if you can picture and imagine being at your favourite beach on a lovely sunny day. It doesn't matter if you can't get a clear picture in your mind of the beach, just thinking about it is fine too. I'd like you to imagine the beach is completely deserted.

There's just you and you're completely safe and secure and enjoying those peaceful feelings that you can feel in your body. Perhaps you are sitting on the sand or maybe lying down on a rug or a towel, just gazing out towards the ocean. I'm not sure if you can smell the salt air or maybe it's the sound of a seabird calling out faintly in the distance, or perhaps it's just the lovely golden glint of the sunlight off the tops of the gentle waves that really help you to relax here now the most.

As you settle yourself down there, becoming even more comfortable, perhaps you become entranced by the hypnotic motion of the waves as they gently wash against the shore. As I count each wave in turn, you'll find it easier and easier to become so entranced in this beautiful scene that, as I get closer and closer to zero, your mind just seems to float away you'll go even deeper into a lovely enjoyable hypnotic trance.

Ten – As you hear the whoosh of the wave as it washes against the sand on the beach, it's almost as if that wave has washed through you, deep inside, relaxing you and releasing you.

Nine – The next gentle wave washes over you now as you begin to feel deeply calm sensations beginning to flow inside your body

Eight – Another gentle wave slowly advances towards the beach gently washing away stresses and tensions within

Seven – Yet another gentle wave flows over you now, a wave of peace, calm, release, relaxation, taking you down deeper into blissful, peaceful relaxation now.

Six – How lovely it is as you just allow the next wave to gently soothe your busy mind, slowing down thoughts, slowing, releasing, relaxing more now

Five – The sun is so warm and beautiful there and the next wave is so refreshingly warm too, a lovely sensation against your skin which makes you appreciate the beauty of this scene as you relax even deeper now

Four – Each lovely wave takes you deeper now as it caresses your skin and calms the very essence of your spirit deep down inside of you

Three – You become even more aware of more relaxed sensations now perhaps you're deeply aware of your slow relaxed breathing now, or perhaps how your muscles have become so loose and limp and lazy, or perhaps it's your quiet mind that tells you that you are deeply enjoying this hypnotic motion of these lovely waves

Two – Each wave taking you so deep into this beautiful, luxurious, sensuous relaxation that you are beginning to enjoy sooooo much now.

One – Nearly at your perfect level of hypnotic relaxation now as all these lovely feelings continue to intensify with every word I say now.

Zero – So nice to be there now at your perfect level of deep hypnotic relaxation without a single care in the world, free to enjoy being this deeply relaxed now.....that's right....continue to enjoy this perfect level of deep relaxation for the rest of the session.

Deepener No. 3 – Subliminal Deepener

(This could be a good deepener to use with those who seem to be a bit too logical in their thinking or for those who have difficulty in visualising)

There are so many things that we all forget, aren't there? (wait for response)

Here's an example – can you remember what you had for dinner on this day last month? No? Of course you can't. That's right. I can't either. That makes two of us. And I'm pretty such that's the same for just about everybody, isn't it? (wait for response). That's right.

So that means you're pretty good at forgetting things, doesn't it? (wait for response). That's right. In a moment, I going to give you a really simple instruction which is going to help you to go deeper into trance so that you'll enjoy this hypnotic experience even more. So what I'd like you to do now is to consciously forget the instruction I am about to give you.

The reason I want you to consciously forget the instruction I am about to give you is so that it's forgotten consciously so that it becomes an even stronger instruction to your subconscious mind. Is that ok with you? (wait for response)

Good. The instruction that I want you to consciously forget now is that every time I touch the back of your left hand, you'll just go deeper without having to figure out how or why. It'll just happen instantaneously because you've consciously forgotten it while unconsciously remembering it even more strongly so that it happens instantaneously.

So I'd like you to go ahead now and consciously forget what I've just said. When I tap you gently in the middle of your forehead, it'll seem as if that instruction just falls out of your conscious mind as you forget it now. (Tap the client gently in the middle of the forehead with one of your fingers).

(Continue speaking to the client now about whatever you want the client to do or visualise next. Without making verbal reference to it and without advance warning, every so often, touch the client on the back of the hand as you have told them you would. Doing this five or six times generally has the desired effect of deepening the trance sufficiently).

Testing The Level Of Trance
Now that you've successfully done your induction and deepener, you client should be in a nice level of trance. But how exactly do you know if they are actually in trance or just sitting there with their eyes closed wondering when you'll shut up so they can open their eyes again?

Well the answer to that is quite simple really. If you want to know how deeply in trance your client is – just ask. I know that might seem jaw-droppingly obvious, but you'd be surprised how many hypnotists and even professional hypnotherapists forget to ask. I know there have been times I've even forgotten to, although, thankfully, those happened mostly back when I started hypnotizing people first. I had so much on my mind that I was trying to remember back then that it was easy to forget to test for the level of trance.

Trance is a subjective thing. It's really about what your client believes at that moment. From experience, I would say that if a client believes they are in trance then they probably are and are likely to follow your instructions easily, but if the client is doubtful as to whether they are in trance or not, they will prevent themselves from fully enjoying it and going deeper and may resist your suggestions or even begin to come out of trance.

Because trance is subjective, when we test, we tell the client in various different ways that suit the client, that they can measure how relaxed they are on a scale. That scale could be zero to ten or zero to one hundred (or whatever you choose). If a client tells me before going into trance that their most relaxed place is watching tv, I'll ask them to imagine a scale appearing on the tv with a moveable marker that can slide up or down to indicate how relaxed they are right now.

I'll tell them that ten represent when they are full aware and fully conscious and zero represent how relaxed they are when they are engrossed in their favourite tv show. I then ask them to tell me where they are on the scale right now.

If they aren't quite at zero, I'll tell them that where they are right now is just perfect and with each breath they take, they can see or feel that scale moving ever closer to zero as they relax even more with each easy breath they take or perhaps with every soothing word I say.

Keep going with this until your client reaches zero. Remember, it's their experience, not yours, and they can choose to go into hypnosis at the rate that suits them. Keep asking them every so often where they are on the scale. Each time you ask them where they are on the scale now, phrase it like this - "how much closer to zero are you now?". This pre-supposes that they are continually getting closer and closer to zero and will help them to relax even more.

So now you've done your induction successfully, you've done your deepener successfully and you've tested for the level of trance and you've gotten your client to zero. Wonderful. Well done! Now you need to understand what's happening in your clients experience. Trance level can fluctuate and the client can go deeper than you intended.

So How Deep Can Your Client Go?

There are a number of so-called different scales of depth of hypnosis. It is important to recognise that a scale of depth of hypnosis is a guide only and each hypnosis experience is subjective and individual. The following scale is what's known as the Aron's Scale and is the one that, in my opinion, is the most useful.

Stage 1: HYPNOIDAL – Very light stage of hypnosis in which most clients don't feel hypnotized. The majority of people feel completely awake. Two types of HYPNOIDAL states are Hypnopompic and Hypnagogic. Hypnopompic is the state by before waking up in the morning and Hypnagogic is the state right before falling asleep at night. Weight reduction, smoking cessation and simple muscle control such as eyelid catalepsy are easily achieved at this stage.

Stage 2: More relaxed state where larger muscle groups can be controlled and manipulated such as Arm Catalepsy. Your power of critical reasoning starts to become less apparent.

Stage 3: You get fairly complete control of your entire muscular system. Most people won't be able to articulate a number, stuck to a chair, can't walk and even partial analgesia.

Stage 4: In this stage you start to produce greater phenomena and is known as the beginning of the amnesic stages. Your client will actually forget items such as their name, number, address and other items. Glove Analgesia and feeling touch, but no discomfort.

Stage 5: This is considered the start of somnambulism. You can experience complete anesthesia and experience the ability to neither feel discomfort or touch. A lot of different pain control techniques can be used in this stage as well. You can also experience what is called Positive Hallucinations which means you can see and hear things which do not actually exist.

Stage 6: This is the next level of Profound Somnambulism. You can experience negative hallucinations which means you won't see or hear things that actually do exist.

One of the most striking examples I had of profound somnambulism (Stage 6) was a lady who came to see me for a particular food addiction that she wanted to overcome. I did a standard progressive relaxation induction with her because she performed really well during the suggestibility tests. I deepened with a simple counting from 10 down to 1, and she showed all of the signs of becoming more and more relaxed - her breathing slowed, her skin tone changed, her lower lip became a little more swollen and she very easily forgot things such as numbers, etc.

She went so deep so fast that I was delighted. And then I started to ask for her responses, so I'd ask her to imagine something for me and then respond by saying ok. She didn't respond. So then I asked the question in another way. She still didn't respond. I tried using her name a lot. She still didn't respond.Then I switched to ideomotor signalling (you'll learn all about this in the next chapter). I asked her to just raise the first finger of her left hand if she could hear my voice. She didn't respond!

At this stage, I was starting to think "oh hell, why do I have to be the first hypnotist in the history of the world to have a client get stuck in hypnosis?" Now, of course, that's nonsense and it's never happened and it couldn't happen in this situation either, but for a split second the thought still ran through my mind.

I then decided to end the trance, so I brought her out of trance and then quickly put her back into trance but suggested that she would only go to a level where she could continue to hear and respond to my voice. That didn't work either!

At this stage, I was no longer worried - I was just frustrated. So I brought her out of hypnosis again and took a little longer before I put her back into hypnosis again and tried again. Still no joy. I tried ideomotor signalling (next chapter) again. That didn't work either!

I asked her that same bloody question about 100 times and then, out of the blue, 55 minutes after beginning, she began responding perfectly, and we continued with the session as if nothing had happened. The funny thing is, I asked her later about what she experienced when I asked her that first question. I asked her if she was aware of taking some time to answer.

To my amusement, she said "No. I think I answered straight away, maybe within about 30 seconds of when you asked me the question". She had no recollection of going in and out of trance. Needless to say, when I told her it was actually 55 minutes before she responded, she thought I was lying to her! It's at times like that I wish I had the session video recorded so that I could prove it.

You'll be rather glad to know that was the only client I've had like that in the past three years and I regularly see between 20 and 30 people per week. I think the learning to take from that story is that every client is different and will respond differently. When you become really elegant at doing hypnosis, you'll just flow with the client and deal with whatever happens in front of you.

My best advice is, when something doesn't work in the way you expect, do something else. Most people tend to fall into the first category (Stage 1) where they come out of hypnosis and aren't really too sure if they have been in hypnosis. This is why it's important to explain hypnosis really well beforehand, to test for hypnosis and then if the client says afterwards that they weren't sure if they were in hypnosis, ask them about how they would explain not being able to open their eyes, the level they said they were at, etc.

This is not about "conning" the client into believing they have been in hypnosis. This is about pointing out the hypnotic phenomena that they have actually experienced. By pointing these out and getting the client to realise they have actually been in hypnosis (no matter how light), you are increasing the likelihood that they'll experience even better hypnosis the next time.

So, What Have You Learned?
Time to test your retention again.
1. Why is it a good idea to deepen trance?
2. What's the reason for wanting the client to be convinced that they were in hypnosis?
3. What's the name of the scale used to determine the level of trance your client is experiencing?

If you've answered those questions correctly, well done. As with hypnotic inductions, I would also strongly recommend you learn by heart at least one of these deepeners. Once again, it's all about looking and sounding confident as you are guiding a person into hypnosis. In the next chapter, you'll learn how to get your client to respond to you while they are in trance.

Chapter Eight

Eliciting Responses In Trance

<u>Learning Outcomes From This Chapter</u>
- You'll learn how your client responds in hypnosis
- You'll learn what ideomotor signalling is
- You'll learn when it is appropriate to use ideomotor signalling
- You'll learn what clean language is and how to use it
- You'll learn about utilization and how to incorporate it into your hypnosis session

Ok, so now you have your client in hypnosis, you've deepened and you've tested to make sure your client is really enjoying their perfect state of relaxation – now what? Well now that your client is in hypnosis, you've got to learn how to get responses and how to use clean language. (When I say clean language, I don't mean that you avoid cursing. Clean language means something entirely different in hypnosis!)

How A Client Responds

How clients respond when they are in hypnosis is interesting. I recommend that you keep the focus of your gaze on your client at all times so that you notice even the slightest little changes. We'll refer to this a bit more towards the end of this chapter when we learn about utilization.

One of the first things to notice about how your client responds. If they respond a bit too quickly, that could mean that their conscious mind is still actively listening and has the potential to get in the way of any suggestion you will make later. Your task then is to continue with maybe a confusional technique to get the conscious mind out of your way.

I would regularly go through the induction – deepener – testing process fine and then find that when my client is responding, they may answer a question a bit too quickly. This just means that I've been doing fine up until that point and maybe the conscious mind has become just a little more active again and I'll immediately use some confusional technique or extra deepening technique that gets the conscious mind to go away again.

In my experience, trance depth can come and go – it doesn't have to remain at a medium level once you've achieved that at the start and you have to be alert to this and just be aware that every so often, it may be necessary to do a little more deepening, depending on the client.

Clients can respond by talking – saying things out loud, or, if they are really relaxed, they may not be all that inclined to speak. If so, it is rather handy to be able to use ideomotor signals.

What Is Ideomotor Signalling?

Ideomotor signals can be explained really simply – they are just a way to get your client to respond non-verbally. Our unconscious minds – that part of us responsible for automatic emotional responses – processes things more in images or metaphors.

To put it simply, a person who has a panic attack in the middle of a supermarket logically knows there is nothing dangerous there - they can even verbalise those logical thoughts but that still doesn't prevent them from having a panic attack. When the client doesn't have to go through the arduous process of translating a thought into understandable language, we can establish a very effective communication with the unconscious part of the mind.

Here's an example of how you would get the unconscious to establish an ideomotor signaling system:

"I would like your unconscious to select a finger to signify yes. When it has selected that finger, allow that finger to move a bit, just like as if it's twitching. (Wait until you see a finger twitch.)

Thank you. That's great. Now, I would like you're unconscious to select a different finger to signify no. When it has selected that finger, once again, let that finger move so I know which one it is. (wait until you see a finger twitch). That's great, You're doing really well there. I'd like your unconscious to remember which fingers it's selected (your _____ finger means yes, and your _____ finger means no. Very good."

Now you can begin to ask the unconscious questions. Keep re-stating which finger means yes and which means no as you ask questions. You should stick to relatively simple questions which can attract a yes or no answer.

When Is It Appropriate To Use Ideomotor Signalling?
Ideomotor signaling can achieve great results in the following areas
  • Getting a commitment from the unconscious mind to do something or to resolve something.
  • Finding things that you may have lost or misplaced
  • Finding root causes of things that happened to you
  • Remembering certain things or feelings that the client knows deep down but may just be unable to remember consciously.

Remember not to go too far here. A trained therapist knows how to use these techniques to help a client achieve powerful emotional change relating to an emotional or anxiety-related issue. If you have no training in this area, steer clear for now. Just stick to simple yes or no answers in relation to trivial things such as items that have been lost or misplaced.

If you do venture into using this technique in order to try to help a client to overcome a deep-seated emotional issue without having the appropriate training, you risk getting a reaction that you do not know how to deal with and you risk making your client feel worse rather than better.

What Is Clean Language?
Whenever I mention using clean language to a person who is eager to learn hypnosis, it is always greeted with a raised eyebrow or a grin. And of course it's natural to assume that the opposite of clean language is dirty language which to most of us means cursing. And of course you're not going to curse at your client! At least I hope you're not anyway!

What I mean by clean language is phrasing your language very carefully in order not to lead your client. If you ever watch courtroom drama's on TV, you may see an attorney asking a question of a witness such as "So Ms. X, who was with you on that night in the factory?". And then you'll hear the opposing lawyer quickly saying "Objection.....leading the witness".

This is an ideal example of what I mean. The first attorney was assuming that there was someone else with Ms. X. If you are to use clean language, you attempt (in as much as is possible), not to lead or assume. So, in the example above, if the attorney was using clean language, he might say "Ms. X, on that night in the factory, to your knowledge, was there anyone else in the factory?". You might think it's a subtle difference and you'd be right. It is.

However, it is really important in hypnosis, because when a client is in hypnosis, we are dealing with their unconscious imaginative mind rather than their logical analytical mind. When you lead the unconscious mind, it can come up with scenario's that might not be true in order to satisfy the leading instruction it has received.

Some questions which aren't "clean -
- "So, what is the problem?" - this assumes there is a problem.
- "How can I help you?" - this assumes the client needs help
- "How did your father affect you?" - this assumes the father did have an effect

"Clean" alternatives
- "What exactly is it that you want?" - focusses the client on their preferred outcome

- "How do you want that to happen? - focusses the client on outcome
- "Was there anything from your childhood that may have a bearing on this outcome in any way?".allows the client permission to refer to their childhood if they feel its appropriate

I'm not really going to explore clean language in too much detail here. There are some excellent books on the subject where you'll find a lot more information on the subject. All that's necessary for the purposes of this book is that you are aware that how you phrase your questions or comment can taint the response you get.

What Is Utilization?
Utilization is a term that was coined by Milton Erickson who was known as the father of modern hypnosis. Erickson showed us that if we actually use every response of the client, every sound in the background, every sensation that happens, etc, we can help the client to go into a really nice state of hypnosis. Probably the best way to describe this is to use and example.

In a previous house of mine, one of my next door neighbours had an unnaturally loud lawnmower. This was quite literally the loudest lawnmower I have ever heard! And she had a habit of mowing her lawn about once every second day. As I was seeing clients in an office at the side of my house, you'd imagine this was a big problem.

A typical situation might be that I'd done my induction, the client was relaxing nicely and then I'd move into my deepener and suddenly, out of the blue, this thunderous noise would start up. And I can honestly say, if I didn't know about utilisation, I would have ended up with no clients!

All I simply did was to say something like this - "that's right, and now there's even the sound of a lawnmower in the background which reminds you so nicely of lazy hot summer days where all your worries and cares just seem to melt away. That sound will just help you to go deeper and deeper and it's throbbing monotonous tone quickly seems to just fade into the background as you go deeper and deeper...."

So, in other words, you use whatever the client is experiencing, feed it back to them and suggest that it'll help them to go deeper. Acknowledge it and use it to help them go deeper. If your client coughs, acknowledge it and use it. If they move around a bit, use it. If they sigh, or take a deeper breath, use it.

There are so many things that happen in our experiences ranging from subtle to really obvious (like that lawnmower), but if you use them correctly, they'll your client to achieve a really nice hypnotic state.

It doesn't have to be only at the induction stage that you use this. You can continue to utilize all the way through the session. So if the client smiles at the mention of something you describe, then mention it. Perhaps you'd say something like - "that's right, that little smile there can remind you of so many other times you have felt this good...." or something along those lines.

So, What Have You Learned?
Here are some questions to see just how well you have learned the information in this chapter.

1. What do you need to do in order to know how the client is responding?
2. What are ideomotor signals?
3. What is utilization?

If you have gotten this far and you have practised everything you've learned so far, you're doing really well. Now its time to add in some suggestions.

Chapter Nine

Post-Hypnotic Suggestions

<u>Learning Outcomes From This Chapter</u>
- How Do I Structure A Good Post Hypnotic Suggestion?
- Why Don't PHS's Work All The Time?
- What s Trance Depth & Why Is It Important?
- Does a PHS Work Best If The Client Can't Remember It?

There are a number of simple but very important rules to follow in order to structure a good post-hypnotic suggestion.

Suggestions Should Be Positive – it is best to completely eliminate any negative language should as "not" or "can't". In other words, a suggestion such as "you'll not feel stressed" is not the greatest of suggestions while "you are calm and in control at all times" is much better

Suggestions Should Be In The Present Tense – for instance if you tell the client "you will feel calm and relaxed when you are on that aeroplane", there is an emotional disconnect because you are not asking them to do anything right now. If you ask them to project into the future and "be there" on the aeroplane and then you say "now you feel calm and relaxed", this is much more effective.

Suggestion Should Be Achievable – suggestions such as "you are going to win the lottery" will just not work (unless a massive fluke happens). However, a suggestion such as "you are becoming more self-confident every day" is much more achievable.

Suggestions Should Be Meaningful – if a suggestion is too vague or if the client doesn't personally connect with it, it is likely to be less successful. The more personally meaningful a suggestion, the more likely it is to be successful.

Suggestions Should Be Delivered Well – the confidence in your tone of voice and the meaningfulness with which suggestions are delivered will have a positive effect on the success of your suggestions. This means that the assumption that a hypnotist should use a monotone voice is not entirely true, especially not for the post hypnotic suggestion!y

Why Don't Post Hypnotic Suggestions Work All The Time?

This is the subject of much debate and there are any number of reasons why a post-hypnotic suggestion may not work. The main reasons are -

- Suggestions not being constructed according to the guidelines above
- Lack of rapport between client and hypnotist
- Secondary gain – the client may have a better reason to do something different

- Suggestions that are against the clients values or belief systems

The key to making sure your post-hypnotic suggestions work is to test them. So, in other words, the moment a client comes out of hypnosis, test to make sure your post hypnotic suggestion has worked. Let's take an example to illustrate what I mean.....

I would regularly give my clients a post hypnotic suggestion to go deeply into trance when I say the word "Sleep" and touch their shoulder. The reason is that I want to save some time the next time they go into hypnosis, so that I don't have to go through the same long induction / deepener process as the first time.

Then I'll terminate the trance and return them to their full awareness and maybe say a couple of things to them so they have time to re-orient themselves. Then I'll put my hand on their shoulder and say the word "Sleep" loudly and authoritatively. The moment their eyes close and they fall into hypnosis, I'll immediately give them very rapid suggestions to go deeper.

Then I'll terminate trance again and maybe test it again, just to be sure. When I have successfully tested out the post-hypnotic suggestion two or three times, then I'll terminate trance again and let the client leave. If I've done my job really well, they'll go into trance a week later by the same method. All I'll have to do is put my hand on their shoulder and say the word "Sleep".

You may be wondering why I put my hand on their shoulder – well lets just say all I do is tell them that every time they hear the word "sleep", they'll go deeply into hypnosis. And then they are driving their kids to school the next morning and some guy on the radio says the word "Sleep". That might just be kind of dangerous (and a very good way to get sued).

Why Is Trance Depth Important For A PHS To Work?

There are many so-called "scales of hypnosis" out there, and many that have really overcomplicated the whole issue. The reason I say this is because the depth of trance is not as important as what you are going to do with the person once they are at that level of trance. I'm going to give you some examples below to illustrate what I mean.

At one time only three levels of trance depth were reckoned to be important -- light, medium, and deep. Now that's probably fine if all you are doing is having some fun with hypnosis and maybe just doing some deep relaxation or something like that. It becomes a little more important to have a proper scale of hypnosis to be able to test against in order to be able to extract a tooth while under hypnosis alone, or how about performing surgery on a person while using hypnosis instead of anaesthetic, or how about hypnobirthing (this is where the mother opts for a natural birth and goes through hypnosis training in preparation for the birth to enable it to be a much less painful experience).

When you consider some of these applications of hypnosis, it would be kind of important to know that your client is actually experiencing the correct level of hypnosis to allow them to successfully complete those procedures.

Here is a simple and easy guide so that you can understand a little better – remember we referred to the Aron's Scale a little earlier in Chapter 7? Well here's a brief synopsis of the different stages.

Stage 1: HYPNOIDAL – Very light stage of hypnosis in which most clients don't feel hypnotized.

Stage 2: More relaxed state where larger muscle groups can be controlled and manipulated such as Arm Catalepsy. Your power of critical reasoning starts to become less apparent.

Stage 3: You get fairly complete control of your entire muscular system. Most people won't be able to articulate a number, stuck to a chair, can't walk and even partial analgesia.

Stage 4: Your client will actually forget items such as their name, number, address and other items. Glove Analgesia and feeling touch, but no discomfort.

Stage 5: This is considered the start of somnambulism. You can experience complete anesthesia and experience the ability to neither feel discomfort or touch. A lot of different pain control techniques can be used in this stage as well. You can also experience what is called Positive Hallucinations which means you can see and hear things which do not actually exist.

Stage 6: This is the next level of Profound Somnambulism. You can experience   negative hallucinations which means you won't see or hear things that actually do exist.

Here's a brief summary of the type of hypnotic phenomena you'll witness at the various different stages of hypnosis.

Catalepsy
In the first three stages, you will see muscular inability in varying degrees.

Anmesia

In the third stage, you will see some inability to articulate a number, for example. In the fourth stage, you will totally forget a number and not be able to articulate it.

Anesthesia

In the fourth stage of trance depth, you will feel analgesia -- no pain but some pressure. During the fifth stage you will have anesthesia, feeling neither pain nor pressure.

Hallucinations

During the fifth and sixth levels of hypnotic trance, there will first be positive hallucinations of seeing and hearing what actually is not there. In the sixth level, you will not see or hear what actually is there.

For most hypnosis and for doing your own self hypnosis, the light stages are all that you need to accomplish behavior changes.

Does A PHS Work Best If A Client Can't Remember It?

There is some debate on this issue but in my own experience, a post-hypnotic suggestion does work best if the client cannot remember it. That way, when they suddenly find themselves doing whatever it is I have suggested afterwards, they seem to just integrate it into their normal behaviour quicker and easier.

In order to achieve the forgetting of a post-hypnotic suggestion, the client needs to be in a relatively medium state of hypnosis, around a Stage Four on the Aron's Scale mentioned earlier in this chapter.

When delivering the suggestion, you need to be completely confident and assertive in the tone of your voice so that your clients subconscious will not detect any hint of doubt. Remember, even in hypnosis, a client interprets the world through the remaining senses and is perfectly capable of sensing doubt or indecisiveness which, in my opinion, cause the conscious mind to intervene and make a judgement about the post-hypnotic suggestion.

This will also, of course, disturb the level of hypnosis because up until this point the conscious mind has been floating off in some nice little dreamworld. When the mind detects or senses incongruence (in other words, a hint of something that doesn't sit well with the actual suggestion), it can summon the conscious mind back into action momentarily and this will negatively impact the effectiveness of the post-hypnotic suggestion.

After I have tested to be sure the client is at around stage four on the Aron's scale, here's the general form or words I would use to encourage a client to consciously forget a post-hypnotic suggestion -

"Now that you this deeply relaxed, you can appreciate how easily your conscious mind forgets. Perhaps you can remember some amusing experiences where you forgot things and I'm sure there have been many times you have forgotten things. How about what you had for lunch three weeks ago on a Thursday, or who texted you five days ago at 3pm, or perhaps what exact time you woke up on a Saturday morning this time last month? You forget so well, don't you. You have a real talent for it.

So does every human being on the planet. We all forget so easily, and I'd like you to forget the suggestion I am about to give you so that your unconscious mind can absorb it into your behaviour immediately.

Forgetting it consciously makes it much more powerful at an unconscious level. And you'll find it completely acceptable to you to forget it because this suggestion is for your higher benefit and is exactly what you want to happen in your life from this moment forward for the rest of your life.#

After I've told you the suggestion, you'll immediately erase it from your conscious mind, as if I had never mentioned it, and you'll notice that it becomes automatically absorbed into your unconscious mind and from this moment forward, you'll find yourself just doing exactly what I suggest without having to consciously think about it – it'll just happen automatically.

And that thing I'd like you to forget is ...

Now erase it. Right now. Just let it drop out of your mind, so that no matter how hard you try, you just cannot recall what I've just said."

So, What Have You Learned
Time to test yourself again.
1. List three things that suggestions should be.
2. What is secondary gain?
3. At what level of trance would you expect a client to hallucinate?

Now we need to learn how to terminate trance properly.

Chapter Ten

Trance Termination

Learning Outcomes From This Chapter
- You'll Learn How To Terminate Trance Properly
- You'll Learn Two Sample Terminations
- You'll Learn Why It's Important To Terminate Trance Slowly
- You'll Learn What To Do If It Doesn't Work First Time

Terminating trance is something that should be undertaken with care. First of all, lets talk about how not to do it. Imagine for me what it would be like to be asleep or maybe napping, completely unaware of anything going on around you. Then imagine someone else, maybe a friend or your partner, bangs a pot or a pan against a counter-top and wakes you abruptly.

Has that ever happened to you? Have you ever been woken abruptly like that? If you have, do you remember how it felt? Quite uncomfortable, wasn't it? It happened me once and I remember feeling disoriented and almost dazed for the first thirty seconds or so. Not a very nice experience and one that I really wasn't in a hurry to repeat.

When we think about how we would prefer to awaken from sleep or from a nap, it would be slowly and easily. Have you ever had a lazy day where you didn't have to go to work or have anything much to do? On that morning, did you wake up slowly, at your own pace? It was nice, wasn't it?

For the person in hypnosis, it's just the same. They don't want to be startled out of their trance – they'd much prefer to return to their full awareness at a nice, easy pace. Being aware of this can help ensure that person will go into hypnosis even easier the next time. Why? Because they've enjoyed the experience, of course.

How To Terminate Trance Properly

You should take either slightly less than or slightly more than a minute to terminate trance. This way, the client returns to their full awareness slowly and comfortably. Notice I use the words "return to full awareness" rather than "awaken". The reason I do this is to distinguish the hypnotic trance from sleep.

Especially if your client has been in a deep state of hypnosis and you mention the word "awaken", the client can come out of trance believing they were actually asleep and not in trance at all. This can plant seeds of doubt in the mind of the client and could cause them to lessen the effect of the post-hypnotic suggestions you have given them.

Your tone of voice is also very important during the termination of trance. Change the tone of your voice during termination. What I mean by this is that if you are using a pleasant monotone up until termination, then during termination, perhaps quicken the pace of your delivery, use a slightly louder voice and speak with a little more authority.

Now when I say a little more authority, that does not mean barking orders at your client – it just means a slight but noticeable difference. Remember your client picks up on all of these non-verbal instructions and communication.

With clients that are in a very deep state of hypnosis, I have sometimes found that I may have to repeat the termination with even more authority in my voice. I once had a client who needed the termination repeated five times.

The reason I tell you this is so that you do not panic if it doesn't always work out exactly as planned. Sometimes it doesn't and you just have to adapt, without letting your client sense that you are now a bit nervous because the trance termination didn't work the first time. If in doubt, just repeat and change something about what you do or say.

There are some tips and tricks that I have learned through the years about what to do when all else fails. I think the most important thing to remember is that, if a termination doesn't work first time, it's actually a bit of a compliment to your ability to get your client to such a lovely, enjoyable level of hypnosis that do not want to return just yet.

One of the tips I learned is to use the clients name more often the next time your repeat your termination. Keep repeating the clients name constantly throughout your next termination sequence and notice that it gently jogs the client out of trance.

Alternatively, (and this is something I would only use as a last resort), I would try blowing gently on the clients eyelids. This tends to interrupt the enjoyable nature of the trance and guides the client towards terminating the trance. The great news is that these experiences are few and far between, but it's important that you know about them on the off-chance that you will actually come across one.

And remember, the very worst thing that could possibly happen is that your client will drop off into a deep and natural sleep. And if that's the very worst it could get, then it's not that big a deal, is it?

Two Sample Terminations
To help you get started, I have included the following two sample trance terminations, and I recommend that you learn these by heart. As time goes by you may begin to experiment with your own form of words if you'd like, or you could just stay with one of these terminations – it's up to you!

Sample Termination No.1
Each time you go into hypnosis from now on, it'll be easier and quicker to go into trance. In a moment, I'm going to count up from one to five and as I count, with each number, you'll return more and more to your full awareness. When I reach the count of five, your eyes open and you are fully aware again.
Here we go....
One – slowly, calmly and really easily beginning to return to your full awareness
Two – you notice how your muscles and nerves are soooo deeply relaxed
Three – every cell of your body feels perfect, refreshed and re-invigorated
Four – eyelids fluttering now, nearly ready to open

On the next number, your eyes open, you are fully aware and energised.

Five – eyelids open now, fully aware and having a nice big stretch, that's right.

Sample Termination No.2
Take a moment now to review and absorb all of the positive changes you are making today. When that process is completed you can trust your unconscious mind to make all of those changes so you can resist all temptation to try to analyse or understand what we have done in trance.

When all of that has been completed, raise the first finger of your right hand (or left hand)to let me know you are ready to return to your full alert awareness. (Wait for finger signal....). Now I am going to count to five and by the time I reach five you'll be back to your full alert awareness.

One - beginning to leave the trance world behind
Two - returning slowly and gently to your full awareness
Three - your whole body now feeling really good now, really rested and refreshed
Four - your mind returning to full awareness now, eyelids just beginning to open
Five - eyelids wide open now - that's right - fully aware now

Difficult Termination
You may find that some clients enjoy the state of hypnosis so much that they actually don't want to return to their full awareness. And of course, some may have drifted off to sleep. If you are inexperienced at directing hypnotic experiences, you may imagine that if this happened to you (as the hypnotist), that you might panic or not know what to do.

As a veteran of many thousands of hypnotic inductions I can tell you that in the vast majority of cases, it is possible to get your client back to full awareness pretty quickly but you may have to change tack a little bit to achieve this.

The most important thing to remember is that the worst thing that can ever happen is that the client will just drift off to sleep if they are not sleeping already. So there's no need to panic!

Here are a couple of things you can try:
- Raise your voice a little more and use a more authoritative tone of voice
- Say the persons first name more often.
- Blow gently on the persons eyelids
- If all else fails, gently shake the person

So, What Have You Learned?
Lets see how much information you actually retained.

1. Why would it be better to use the term "return to full awareness" rather than "awaken"?
2. Why use more authority in your voice during a termination?
3. Why would you use the persons name more often during a termination?

Chapter Eleven

Final Thoughts

My own journey in learning this phenomenally powerful tool called hypnosis has been fascinating, absorbing, exciting and never-ending. At the beginning of my studies I thought I'd eventually reach a stage where I would know it all.

Now, many years on, I know that this is a journey without an end. But that's pretty cool actually! It means I will never get bored or complacent. I hope that hypnosis does that for you too because since I discovered hypnosis, my own life has become so much better and happier.

Before I discovered hypnosis, I was a total stress-head. I would even go as far as to say I was a stress-junky. The problem was that me doing stress didn't exactly work for the people who were around me at that time. Now, I simply don't do stress. I also don't do worry. Ever!!! I have learned how to control my own mind (and my emotions) so much better that I used to be able to do.

Many people who buy books on how to hypnotize other people do it out of a sense of fascination and observing other people changing seems in some way magical. I would encourage everyone who reads this book to consider using hypnosis on themselves to help them to become more relaxed, to de-stress, to overcome fears and phobias, to release emotional blocks to achievement and to just basically help you to become better at being you. Remember, what you think about today becomes who you are tomorrow!

If you remember, in the Preface, at the beginning of this book, I offered you a **FREE HYPNOSIS MP3**. I hope you have taken me up on the offer. If you haven't experienced trance yet for yourself, you really need to. Go to my website right now and download the free track called **DEEP RELAXATION**. Just go to the homepage of my website

www.pauljhunter.com

All you have to do is scroll down until you see the Deep Relaxation cover and in the box next to it, just enter your name and email address and I'll send it to you **TOTALLY FREE**.

As a word of caution, please do not ever use hypnosis to attempt to manipulate or coerce anyone to do anything or think anything against their will. Your client will more than likely reject anything that is contrary to their values and beliefs, and when they come out of hypnosis, may not like you very much for trying to do that. Hypnosis is such a wonderful gift for the human race to enjoy and explore and I always encourage you to use it with the best of intentions.

I feel a deep sense of gratitude to all of the hypnotherapists through the years who have developed the field of hypnosis to the stage it's at today. People like Dave Elman, Milton Erickson, Richard Bandler, John Grinder, Tad James, Trevor Silvester and many others over the years have helped to shape our knowledge of this wonderful therapeutic tool called hypnosis and I strongly urge you to read some of their works and educate yourself further.

You'll find a list of books that I personally have found to be excellent in developing my own knowledge of hypnosis in the Bibliography section.

And finally - I hope you've enjoyed this book and that you've found it useful and informative. I'd really appreciate it if you would leave an honest review of the book on Amazon just to help other to decide whether or not to purchase.

The secret to becoming good at hypnotizing people really is just practice, practice, practice! Happy hypnotizing!!!!

Chapter Twelve

Bibliography

Included below, you'll find a list of books that I found exceptionally informative during my early days of learning hypnosis. Some of these book relate to more advanced topics that might seem more appropriate for someone who is interested in developing into the hypnotherapy field but I think they add to your understanding of what is possible so I think they are worth reading to improve your knowledge and understanding. Be aware though that actual therapy should only be performed with clients after the appropriate training - reading a book does not make you an expert!

Richard Bandler - "Richard Bandler's Guide To Trance-formation: How To Harness The Power Of Hypnosis To Ignite Effortless And Lasting Change" HCI; 46780th edition (September 26, 2008)

C. Roy Hunter - "The Art Of Hypnosis - Mastering Basic Techniques" Crown House Publishing; 3rd edition edition (May 30, 2010)

Tad James - "Hypnosis - A Comprehensive Guide" Crown House Publishing; 1st Ed. edition (April 30, 2000)

Trevor Silvester - "Cognitive Hypnotherapy - What's That About And How Can I Use It?" Troubador Publishing; UK ed. edition (December 1, 2010)

Dave Elman - "Hypnotherapy" Westwood Publishing Company (1970)

Joseph O'Connor & John Seymour - "Introducing NLP - Psychological Skills For Understanding And Influencing People (Neuro Linguistic Programming) Conari Press; Revised edition (May 1, 2011)

About Author

Paul Hunter is a hugely successful Clinical Hypnotherapist based in Cork in the Rep. Of Ireland. In his office in Cork, he sees clients from all over the world and during the past year, clients have flown in from Dubai, the UK and the United States especially to consult with Paul. His clients come from all walks of life and range from celebrities, famous sports people, politicians to accountants, nurses, teachers, etc.

Paul was the adopted son of Margaret & John Hunter and his upbringing was challenging. His adopted father criticised him for everything he ever did. This left Paul with an inferiority complex that took until later in life to understand and overcome. Overcoming this challenge is one of the things Paul credits with helping him to understand his clients perspective better.

Once college life was over, Paul embarked upon a successful career in sales and held positions in various companies starting as a business-to-business sales representative and culminating as Sales Director with a major national company in Ireland. Sales was never where Paul wanted to be and at age 40, he decided to change career.

In 2006, he made the life-changing decision to train as a hypnotherapist and in 2009, he commenced his practice and rapidly became one of Ireland's busiest and most respected therapists. He is fascinated by human potential and in constantly developing his own ability to communicate with his clients in such a way that is immensely helpful to them in overcoming their problems or issues.

More information can be found on www.pauljhunter.com

Also By

Coming in late summer 2022
GET HAPPY NOW – 10 Happiness Self Help Lessons in
How To Be Happy Every Day

Made in United States
North Haven, CT
09 March 2023